The Cynic & the Fool

The Cynic & the Fool

The Unconscious in Theology & Politics

Tad DeLay

Foreword by Kester Brewin

CASCADE *Books* · Eugene, Oregon

THE CYNIC & THE FOOL
The Unconscious in Theology & Politics

Cascade Books
An Imprint of Wipf and Stock Publishers
199 W. 8th Ave., Suite 3
Eugene, OR 97401

www.wipfandstock.com

PAPERBACK ISBN: 978-1-5326-0424-9
HARDCOVER ISBN: 978-1-5326-0426-3
EBOOK ISBN: 978-1-5326-0425-6

Cataloguing-in-Publication data:

Names: DeLay, Tad.

Title: The cynic and the fool : the unconscious in theology and politics / Tad DeLay.

Description: Eugene, OR: Cascade Books, 2017 | Includes bibliographical references.

Identifiers: ISBN 978-1-5326-0424-9 (paperback) | ISBN 978-1-5326-0426-3 (hardcover) | ISBN 978-1-5326-0425-6 (ebook)

Subjects: LCSH: 1. Lacan, Jacques, 1901–1981. | 2. Psychoanalysis. | 3. Theology. | I. Title.

Classification: BF109.L28 D51 2017 (paperback) | BF109.L28 (ebook)

Manufactured in the U.S.A.   06/16/17

For Deven

Contents

Foreword
by Kester Brewin

A few years ago I flew from London to speak at a conference somewhere in the Ozarks, presenting on a book I'd recently published and catching up with some friends too. I'll be honest; for a number of reasons it wasn't a great period in my life, and my aim was pretty simple: to get through my talks, sell whatever books I could, and catch up with some old friends who were also presenting.

Amidst all this, and the heavy drag of jet lag, it was thus something of a surprise to find myself drawn to one of the breakout sessions, and captivated by the content. The presenter was a young student, but one who spoke with a gravity and grace that defied his age. In amongst a program full of rather familiar radical ideas, and in a context where names of great and difficult thinkers were too comfortably bandied around, here was someone who had taken the vast time needed to sit with and inhabit complex ideas, and wrestle from them insights that immediately resonated.

The presenter was Tad DeLay and, as the fates would have it, some months later he flew across the Atlantic the other way and we were gifted some time to spend talking and traveling together. Sadly, this coincided with some difficult waters for him too and, mixing spirits, our conversations moved swiftly from polite debate to things more bloody, visceral, and vital.

Forgive the reminiscence; I mention this because it gets to the heart of why the book you are holding is so important: the fires from which it has been drawn are real. If you feel the searing, uncomfortable heat of the questions posed in these pages, it is because DeLay has felt it too.

Academia can sometimes appear a cold and clinical place. Getting to grips with Lacan's highly complex topography of psychoanalysis, and then

ix

projecting that map onto the theological landscape to generate a dazzling new cartography that offers us a rich set of coordinates by which to read our socioreligious situation has required an extraordinary depth of reading and reflection. But DeLay is that wonderful thing: the clinician who has also suffered the disease. His diagnosis, and hopeful prognosis, come from his intense study, but are intimately coupled with personal experience of what the journey of recovery continues to entail.

That we are in a period of profound dis-ease is obvious. In my own context in London, the sickness is serious: DeLay's thesis has been played out to shocking perfection by powerful cynics. Twisting facts, generating illusions of monsters, creating fear: all of this has led the masses to be played for fools.

But be in no doubt: the political theatre of "Brexit" was a profoundly theological charade. Comic, yes; slapstick, too often, but in the end a tragedy. Hate crimes soared just as financial prospects slumped and, no sooner than the pantomime was over, those who played the main roles all conveniently exited the stage and returned to their leisure.

Now the same show has played out in even more shocking form in the US, with Trump's election on a wave of anti-elitism, followed quickly by retreat on much of the rhetoric that won him the fight and his subsequent selection of the wealthiest White House cabinet ever.

Underneath all the inflammatory speeches, both Brexit and the US election were religious battles, not so much ones about markets and sovereignty as about "the other," about the demands that powerful systems put on us, about the kinds of people that we want to be.

At this top level, politics is fundamentally a theological matter and, as the US girds for Trump's presidency, it is vital that we see it as such. It is not for me to decide from afar whether, with Trump's victory and terrible civil and racial unrest of the past years, the United States is being overrun with cynics who are playing the people for fools. But what I can emphatically say is this: in the terrifying context in which we find ourselves, DeLay's book should be widely read. This is a text that has the potential to tear the scales from people's eyes, to help them see underneath the surface of what is said and understand the far more forceful gravity of the psychological landscape that is powering these movements. In offering this clarity it is, then, ultimately a book that might well light the fires of hope again. "Any theology that has something to say," DeLay writes in his conclusion, "will conflict with the power structures from which it emerges." He is right. Theology *is* conflict, and if it is not, it is mere indulgence, a Band-Aid on a chronic wound.

Fair warning then: you are about to enter a conflict zone. But as you gather your wits and sharpen your senses, know this: nothing less than the battle for theology's soul is what is at stake here, and if the war is to be won, the fallout from this explosive text must be allowed to infect your politics and sense of self too. Yet, as you turn the page and the fire starts, take heart: you are being led by one who I know—from personal experience I count as a privilege—walks each step with both immense courage and a desire for a better world.

Diogenes and Plato

There was an elderly philosopher known throughout ancient Athens called Diogenes the Cynic. The term *cynic* itself was derived from the Greek word for dog, and to be sure the man was a beast for humankind's entertainment. Abrasive, quick-witted, and always ready to disregard every social custom, the erratic teacher had the reputation of a crazed madman with no respect for gods or kings.

Diogenes the Cynic led a life of absolute poverty, for those who offend as a way of life have few friends and little support. He had only arrived in Athens after being exiled, and he survived on the diet of a beggar. One of the very few people who kept him company was the great philosopher Plato, who said Diogenes was like Socrates gone mad. So it was that Plato entered the humble abode of Diogenes the Cynic on a day that was recorded in the history of philosophy.

"My poor friend," Plato began, "you are a dog who lives in abject poverty because of the way you speak. Can you not perceive the way the world works? If you could only learn to bow before the gods, you wouldn't have to subsist on meals of lentils and water!"

The dog clenched his fists around the bowl of food he was preparing to survive another day. A crooked smile spread across his face and his elderly eyes lit.

"My poor friend Plato," Diogenes replied, "do you not perceive the way the universe works? If you could only learn to subsist on lentils and water, you'd never again have to bow before the gods."[1]

---

1. The stories throughout this book about Diogenes are adapted from Dobbin, ed., *The Cynic Philosophers from Diogenes to Julian* and Laertius, *Lives of the Philosophers*.

1 How to Prohibit a Question

It's been said the questioning of religion is the beginning of a flood.[1] We begin with a critical look at the most basic assumptions we've held so close, and in no time we have turned our eyes outward to every suspicious command to see the world a certain way.

The pollsters ask us whether we are of this faith or that, whether we are atheist or agnostic or Christian, and occasionally they ask us if we are spiritual but not religious. They chart our answers upon a graph suggesting a person with belief A will likely hold viewpoints X, Y, or Z. They cast us into groups and make assumptions about those groups. They call the results statistics, sociology, or even anthropology. A survey doesn't care whether we are cynics or fools, so rarely do the pollsters ask, "Do you really have any evidence you believe this, or do you just imagine you do?" Here is another question of intersecting desires they won't ask: why is it that your opinion on the creation stories in Genesis might let me guess what you think of the minimum wage?

In this book, I aim to investigate the dynamics of collective belief, and I'm focusing on two extremes, the cynic and the fool, which I'll explain by the end of this chapter. I'm using these two extremes as a way to think about how we hear the same message and yet adopt diametrically opposed interpretations. I use the language of theology and politics, because we

---

1. I begin this book with an allusion to the man who said "the criticism of religion is the prerequisite of all criticism." He continued, "Thus, the criticism of Heaven turns into the criticism of Earth, the *criticism of religion* into the *criticism of law*, and the *criticism of theology* into the *criticism of politics*." See Karl Marx, "A Contribution to the Critique of Hegel's Philosophy of Right," 1 and 2.

invest these fields with an intense overload of meaning, ritual, symbols, and motion. The overload creates an interpretation filter. As a scholar of philosophy, religion, and psychoanalytic theory, I only consider my work important if it communicates beyond academic boundaries for the good of the public.[2] I'm organizing my themes around this key question: when we hear a claim that cannot possibly be true, (1) is the false claim pouring forth from the misinformed but honest fool, or (2) is the claim being twisted by a cynical nihilist who knows perfectly well how to manipulate and mislead? It is a question filling the nightly airwaves when a pundit—after hearing the most dubious claims imaginable from an extremist during an interview— must decide whether the politician is so foolish as to actually believe what he just said or, instead, is just towing a party line he knows is false. It is an admittedly oversimplified question (for we are always a mix of motives), but I'm arguing this avenue of critical thinking begins to peel off the layers of false consciousness infecting public discourse.

It was a mistake to think of ourselves as *desiring to know*. It would have been far truer to stop the sentence early—we are subjects who *desire*.[3] We are fools by birth, and a few of us ascend into critical thinking or descend into unconcerned cynicism. Wherever our unconscious desires wander, our conscious justifications will follow. We are desiring machines that eat and breathe and heat, and only occasionally do we desire to know any-thing.[4] Why do we depend on key beliefs to give us identity, and why does a belief about one thing indicate something completely unrelated? What are we telling ourselves with the ideas we make so important, and what else might those key ideas tell us about ourselves? In short, why does a belief always hide among others? And as the waters rise, when does a single drop cause the dam to breach?

---

2. I've aimed to make this book as accessible as possible, but those who find this book too simple may enjoy my previous book, *God Is Unconscious*. Throughout *The Cynic & the Fool*, I am admittedly simplifying philosophical and psychoanalytic concepts, many of which are some of the most opaque and complex ideas I've ever encountered. In addi-tion to simplifying theory, I am also avoiding block quotes, name dropping, and several other conventions found in more academic works. It is my sincerest hope this makes for a more accessible work. These ideas are all very personal to me, they have enriched my life, and I hope to communicate them well for the reader.

3. For the insight about being subjects who desire (rather than subjects who desire to know), I am indebted to McGowan, *Enjoying What We Don't Have*.

4. The desiring machine that eats, heats, and breathes (among more vulgar things) is from Deleuze and Guattari, *Anti-Oedipus*, 1.

I am a scholar of religion and a philosopher, and the field of religious studies requires my colleagues and I to spend our days analyzing how groups of people become so deeply invested in symbols, beliefs, characters, and practices that seem so clearly absurd to others. Aside from the personal value in considering how our beliefs shape identity, I am not the first to argue that religious studies is precisely the magnifying lens through which we best understand the political and social world. We study the truth structured like a fiction and the fictions posing as truth. We study groups coalescing into movements precisely by refusing to interrogate ideological commitments. This book was written mostly before the 2016 presidential campaign began, but I have continually returned to the theory I've developed in these pages to make sense of a most unprecedented, divisive, and confounding election.

It was the turbulence of anxiety and affect, the era of anger, and the ominous dawn of post-truth. What a bitter irony that those who spent so many years criticizing the so-called moral relativism of a changing culture were, ultimately, the ones who benefited most from the disregard for reality and the embrace of shameless nihilism.[5] They only wanted power with a certain color, so they did not protest. I was wrong in my assumption of who would win the contest, and I hope I am wrong (though fairly certain I am not) in my judgements concerning the monster who did. The question now occupying the pundits is whether actions coming out of the White House are those of a brilliantly calculating and cynical knave or instead a foolish clown. Aspects of wounded narcissism, pointless aggression, and spiritual emptiness make comprehending moves all the more difficult. But when have we ever learned to ask this question well: cynic or fool? This inquiry has become more critical than at any time in recent memory.

We have all trusted in characters who, in retrospect, did not deserve that trust. And likewise, every culture inevitably trusts charlatans and hucksters, idiots and madmen, scheming tacticians and careless blunderers. Here is something terribly and consistently true about our species: *in every horrific episode of history, aggressive decisions seemed perfectly justified to the culture and class in power at the time.* Whether we were repressing ourselves or slaughtering others, the grotesque choice always postured as acceptable. We became evermore adept at convincing ourselves "This time is different from before when we did the same," for we always charted new excuses to repress and oppress. We always say those who raise the alarm

---

5. I should credit my friend Dr. Phil Snider for this observation.

are overreacting. We are told to limit our criticism, to become a moderate centrist who believes nothing firmly, to respect those who haven't earned it, and to join together under the banner of false unity flown by those who praise the closing of our eyes as a virtue. Let us learn to interrogate motives, let us see what lies in front of us, and let us have ears to hear. We must, because while we are discussing religion or politics in the abstract, people are being harmed.

Our Questions Are Not New

In sixteenth-century Europe, there was a curious myth supposing pictures of Martin Luther, the great Reformation preacher, couldn't burn.[6] The myth emerged when a house burned down, and the only thing left unscathed was a single picture of the Reformer. It was a superstitious world where devils were everywhere and causes were always misunderstood. Luther once casually remarked, "Many regions are inhabited by devils—Prussia is full of them."[7] Was it a statement about demons, or was it instead a primitive way of talking about violence, alcoholism, or mental illness? It matters not. Luther was raised in a copper mining village where devils were known to hide in the depths, tricking poor miners into seeing glittering ore where there was only stone. It was a world in which a sexual dream led the pious sixteenth-century peasant Christians to fear she might have been seduced by a devil during the night. Even at an old age, Luther often told of looking out his window and seeing the devil. In these visions, the devil was always exposing his backside. It is interesting to consider how such a world-changing scholar would have such persistent hallucinations fixated upon the backside of a demon.

In a superstitious world where devils caused mischief, any possibility of warding them off was a precious technology. After the image of Luther didn't burn in one house, people began fixing his portrait to their wall as a form of preventative fire insurance. Rituals and formulas always aim to control anxiety. Would it really matter if the comforting technology actually worked? No, it would only matter that anxiety was kept in check.

6. See Scribner, "Incombustible Luther."

7. Erikson, *Young Man Luther*, 59. Material here and elsewhere on Martin Luther comes largely from Erickson's work. It was a controversial book, but I've found it incredibly helpful. Material on Luther is also significantly indebted to my instruction under Ingolf Dalferth, a scholar whose expertise would be difficult to overstate.

We create entire interconnecting belief networks. We are forever mixing metaphors and facts, opinions and resentments, understandings and misunderstandings. Our species will teach and govern and, on occasion, we examine ourselves. We do our best to avoid analyzing whatever is right in front of us and staring us in the face. We do not desire to know, so we erect our common sense politics, our perfect theologies, and our untouchable traditions. Common sense is what we desperately cling to when we can't be bothered with the facts. We seek out the guardians of Truth and ask them what to believe, and they tell us the solution is *orthodoxy* (from the Greek for "right word"). Of course, orthodoxy is what we desperately cling to when we have nothing to say about the doctrine itself.[8] Do not trust those charlatans who style themselves as the safely orthodox guardians of Truth. They say their unquestionable Truth should have a capital T, because they know they can't defend their positions without the hammer of ignorance. When questions are prohibited, what happens is nothing but chaos. This is a book about the chaos.

We feel a deep need to define everything with precision, because we lack imagination. Certainty is actually a type of ambiguity, and we answer questions ambiguously inasmuch as we are certain the question points to a problem. When we answer a question ambiguously, it is because we are keeping our anxiety at a distance, for anxiety indicates a flaw. When we don't know, the fear is we might be wrong. So instead of seeking knowledge, we befriend certainty, the father of security. Just as the body desires homeostasis, the mind prefers the territory it already knows. We wouldn't admit it, but given the choice between anxious uncertainty and wrongheaded certainty, we'd prefer to stick with the false ideas we already believe. This is because we are human.

None of this is new. The Apostle Paul wrote about this ages ago: "For now we see in a mirror dimly, but then face to face; now I know in part, but then I will know fully just as I also have been fully known."[9] Even when we admit we don't fully know the truth—for to have faith in anything is to admit we're uncertain—there's still the hope we will know eventually. And while we have a desire to know ourselves, it is often those around us who

---

8. I repeat this claim throughout the book, and I am inspired by a particular line, "One remains true to propriety because one has nothing to say about the doctrine itself," in Lacan, *Écrits*, 205.

9. 1 Cor 13:12 (NASB).

know us better than we know ourselves. It's easier not to know our darker impulses.

I don't really need to tell you what I believe, for you can follow me around for a week and then tell me what I believe. You'll see whether or not I care about child labor if you look at the receipts for my purchases. My bank statement would confess whether I donate to charities or spend selfishly. My friends can tell you whether I am fearful or optimistic, full of rage or forgiveness. As the Apostle Paul hints, we only start to learn after admitting we only see as if through a dim and darkened glass. Let's put it this way: in *every* significant idea we ever believe, we are *always* at least partly wrong—100 percent of the time.

Still, this won't stop seekers of certainty from protesting. They will say we have many things of which we can be certain and shouldn't ever doubt, that there are negotiable beliefs and nonnegotiables as well. The psychoanalyst Sigmund Freud observed we make three defenses for why we believe as we do. (1) We say this is simply what our tribe has always believed. Our ancestors believed X, and we have believed X ever since. (2) We may claim we have the proofs for X. We will convince ourselves we have reasons and evidence. (3) Finally, we may tip our hand and admit the honest truth: it was prohibited to ask questions about X. Ignorance is bliss, and questions stir controversy. It's easier to just not ask. Borders are easiest to defend when they are clear and impenetrable, rising into the sky like a great wall telling us where our boundaries lie. And those boundaries do indeed lie.

Which Is the Symptom? Which Is the Cause?

Any of these three explanations for belief might work alone, but when they are combined in scattershot arguments they start to look like one of Freud's favorite jokes. Mr. A. borrowed a kettle from Mr. B., but when the kettle was returned to Mr. B., he saw a hole in the bottom. Enraged over his damaged kettle, Mr. B. decided to confront his friend. Of course, Mr. A. was enraged over getting the blame, and he erupted, "First, I never borrowed a kettle from B. at all; secondly, the kettle had a hole in it already when I got it from him; and thirdly, I gave him back the kettle undamaged!"[10] Does it even matter how much our apologetics and defenses contradict each other? No, not as long as they keep us feeling secure. The need for security is a *symptom*: something isn't working as it should.

10. Freud, *Jokes and Their Relation to the Unconscious*, 62.

The classic question every therapist must ask is: which is the symptom, and which is the cause? A doctor may treat a headache (symptom) with aspirin when the cause is a common cold; the same symptom-treatment alone would be deadly if the cause is cancer. A therapist may treat depression as a symptom of chemical imbalance and prescribe antidepressants, but this will not matter if the true cause is a failed relationship. The computer programmer asks: which problem is a bug in the code, and which problem is actually a feature of the program? The economist must ask: is wealth inequality a symptom of a poor decision, or is it the inevitable result? And when we are prohibited from asking questions—whether the person refusing to answer us is a doctor, a therapist, a television pundit, or a priest—we can be sure our world is lying. Lying is what boundaries do.

The self-righteous might imagine their steadfast faith is a virtue, but there's nothing virtuous in traveling down a crumbling path. I grew up very religious, and this book will bear out the history of how I learned to take ideas more seriously than the simple religious people from my youth. Your stories and mine will doubtlessly cross. I was twenty years old when I first began emerging from the fundamentalism I had inherited. My paradigm shifted around a series of lost beliefs, and those who have experienced the process will know what I mean when I say a paradigm shift is an unexpected and uncontrollable cascading reaction. It is a flood. Here is the first, and it is how I learned to see prohibitions on questions as a type of inverted truth.

I had recently learned the Bible uses the Greek words *hades, gehenna,* and *tartarus,* and that these are translated as hell anywhere from zero to twenty-three times depending on translation. I had also learned none of those Greek words actually means anything close to what we think of as hell, and thus the most accurate translation would contain zero hells. I asked a long-trusted friend and pastor (if any seminary-trained clergyman already knows this) why I hadn't heard this long before. His reply was simple enough, if stifling: "Tad, you should be *beyond* asking this."

He didn't mean beyond in the sense of no longer caring. He meant I should consider the matter settled and think myself above asking such important questions. He didn't mean I should be more sophisticated but instead less. He meant I shouldn't care. Several conversations like this ripped apart my childlike faith in short order, but the moment that finally destroyed the remnants of my dogmatic upbringing was when I took one final question to this same pastor: why don't we feed the poor? To this day, I still admire the consistency in his answer, a remarkable consistency matched only by its brutal disregard for global poverty. He answered me back: "We can afford to supply food or supply missionaries—dying of starvation is nothing when compared to the agony of hell." In a sense, he was right. He was keeping true to the childlike faith I was in the process of betraying. If there is such a thing as hell, only the most brutal among us would spend a dime or moment of life on anything other than the project of saving souls. I appreciate the corrupt morals of this pastor, because they held up a mirror and allowed me to see the rational conclusion of what I too had believed.

If you have changed your mind on a significant idea, then you might know what I mean when I say the paradigm shift often happens in an unexpected flash. You also know (1) you know the other side because it was once yours, and (2) those still on the side of childlike faith or common sense, those who haven't changed their mind, cannot understand their beliefs in the same way you do now. There's a big difference between disagreeing with something outright versus disagreeing with something you once believed, but those who've never awakened cannot understand the difference. They will imagine you've simply not heard a key argument, when in fact the whole problem is that you've heard them all. The idea that fails doesn't necessarily tell you what the truth will be, but it does tell you what the truth will not be. I left the meeting knowing my religious paradigm would never work the same again. I knew his views were not outliers. Those views were consistent with everything else taught in the Evangelical world, which captures one in three people in the United States. Those views are symptoms, but of what? What causes people to find security in the eternal burning of those with different beliefs, with the destruction of the world in an apocalypse, or with the starvation of children? I wasn't supposed to ask, and then I couldn't avoid asking. These views were features of the program, not bugs, and I fell down the lonely path of asking why people believe what they believe.

Most don't ask those questions, and they are those I'm calling *fools*. A smaller and devious group, those unfortunately praised as leaders far too often, would prefer the masses remain foolish. Those devious men (and occasionally women, but it's usually men, yes?) are *cynics*. The cynic is unconcerned with your opinions so long as they don't hamper his efforts. There can be a heroic form of cynicism, one embracing the dangerous terrain of skepticism and seeing through the surrounding lies. I wholly affirm the positive, heroic, skeptical form of cynicism, but this is not what I'm interested in here. When someone says a politician is cynical, they aren't talking about skepticism but instead a disregard for those they will harm.

When I say *cynic* in this book, I mean the version that is uncaring and cruel. I mean something less like perceptiveness and more like nihilism. I mean those who don't care about the truth and use people as means to an end. When I say *fool*, I do not mean stupid but instead those who desire to believe directly, without equivocation, and with genuine trust. I'm using these terms in a specific sense, and I wish for a world where we could believe directly without potential for abusive manipulation. I'm arguing the foolish mode of belief is more honest, but it becomes abused by the cynic. I want to argue we cannot even begin to understand where a train of thought is leading—whether it ascends to the heavens or plunges over a cliff—unless we consider a simple spectrum from cynicism to foolishness.[11]

There are at least three difficulties with using the terms *cynic* and *fool*. The first is semantic, given that I am using these terms in a very specific sense standing outside common usage. If it ever becomes unclear what I mean by these terms, I recommend returning to the previous paragraph. The second difficulty is that I am framing these as a binary, and a good rule of thumb is to always assume an choice between two hides many other options. We are instead a mix of options, and I am using cynic and fool as two extreme ends of a spectrum. The final difficulty is more difficult to defend, but I want to acknowledge it all the same: cynicism is rarely a good thing, and second-guessing another's motives often leads into the same trap. When we say a person has cynical views, we are usually saying they doubt everyone's motives out of anger or discontent. Further, we are often simply wrong when we guess at another's motives and decide they have bad intentions. We are told we should be hopeful and not cloak our cynicism in the guise of realism, practicality, or some other smug identity. These are very real traps we must seriously consider.

This book is about the motives of others and ourselves, and I might err. Put more strongly, there is absolutely no chance we will not, at least occasionally, misjudge. I wholly acknowledge the downside to judging another's motives and the risk of needless negativity. But I also believe we must engage this task. It is not cynical to look and see what lies plainly before us. On the contrary, we are living in a truly hopeless world if we

11. This book is organized around the cynic-fool relationship, so I should credit Jacques Lacan for delivering this idea. He actually uses the word *knave* rather than *cynic*, and he avoids the term *cynic* precisely because cynicism can also mean informed or heroic. I opt for cynic because it is a more common word, but I mean it specifically in the sense of being uncaring, of using people and words alike as means to an end. To read the inspiration for this book, see Lacan, *The Ethics of Psychoanalysis*, 182–83.

cannot look upon those who cause harm and ask why. I want to argue that endless optimism can lead to the worst of all cynicism, a cynicism refusing to see the clandestine motives of those creating chaos. I want to argue that delving into the contradictions between conscious and unconscious motives is ultimately the most hopeful position available. A disease is only cured when a symptom is diagnosed correctly.

I'm arguing the abuses we see throughout religion, politics, and culture all too often follow from the public's desire to directly trust in leaders who see their every move as a means to an end. I'm saying everyone in the room can vocally agree while concealing their differences. I'm claiming priests and preachers, politicians and pundits, and all those who are subjects-supposed-to-know say a great many things they know are false. It isn't such a novel claim, but I am pushing further; they are playing this game because it is the game we demand they play. They imagine we desire deception, and they are right. We should think about how this pattern variously affects the liberal and the conservative, our religion and our politics, and, above all, our curious desire to trust. We are not subjects who desire to know, but we are subjects who desire a subject-supposed-to-know.

Freud's three defenses for our beliefs (our ancestors believed, we have the proofs, or we are prohibited from asking questions) are always rationalizations. The rational mind is like a weak rider trying to control a much more powerful horse, and we are deceived into thinking we are in control.[12] We didn't evolve to consider how we might be wrong about everything. Sometimes a story or two, much like music or a work of art, helps short-circuit the defenses we throw in protest against foreign ideas. So I have interspersed each chapter with a short parable built around the theme of the following chapter. These stories have served me, and now I hope they serve you.

It is, of course, far too simple to say we are either corrupt cynics or instead delusional fools. At every turn, we are a mix of interests just as every priest and politician is a mix of motives. I teach in universities, and I know very well the expectations placed upon the teacher as the subject-supposed-to-know. So here at the beginning of our journey, let me disabuse you of this notion: I don't have the truth mapped out, just as the smug, self-styled guardians of Truth don't have the truth mapped out. The difference between me and them is that I am going to admit up front I do not know

---

12. This example is Freud's, where he pictures the conscious ego (rider) trying to control the unconscious impulses of the id (horse). See Freud, "The Ego and the Id," 636.

where my train of thought will take me in the years ahead. We are always grappling toward the truth, and we strive forward until anxiety rears its head and shows us just how much our world will change should we chase the truth a bit further. I have no interest in convincing you my perspective holds the absolute Truth. That is not the place for books with something to say. I desire to incite something: questioning, doubting, or rethinking on occasion. The point of a book is not to chip away at falsehood but instead to see our active desire for fictions and false consciousness undergirding every question we ever (neglect to) ask. I am interested in the flood of questions that shall cause the dam to breach.

The Prisoner

In the late nineteenth century, there was a brutal murderer who was slated for execution. He would hang from the gallows in a dark British prison, and the guilt of this grotesque monster was beyond dispute. The crowds, so very desperate for justice, gathered outside the prison awaiting the madman's payment for his sins, for those who cannot become like us must be expelled. The world demands the unrighteous pay. It is the way it has always been.

The era was a mix of innovation and brutality. The Industrial Revolution had brought the former, and the Great War would soon bring the latter. It was a time of rapid change and possibilities beyond anything society had ever dreamed, but it was also a time of harsh labor conditions, rampant pollution, and everything else suggesting the world was changing for the worse. Amidst all this, the Church of England was a vestige of a bygone era. Our gods, politics, and public rituals were never supposed to change. Society was built upon confession and execution. It wasn't so very different from our time.

As the condemned man was led out of his prison cell to the gallows, the raucous crowds awaited word the monster's life had ended. This scene was routine, for thousands of death marches before it had always concluded with the uproarious applause, which was followed by silence, which was followed by everyone returning to their homes and going about their day. The schedule was simple: a prisoner, a procession toward the gallows, a priest within the procession, and then the lifeless corpse of the hanged man—a human punishment to surely be followed with a divine punishment.

The unconcerned priest read from his sacred book of the hell awaiting the prisoner, but he also spoke of the consolations sure to follow upon sincere repentance. Of course, if a man repents in the last moment, the execution of a brother in faith would be more difficult to bear. We'd never say it, but we prefer the monster remain a monster to justify our desire for vengeance. The dull and droning warnings from the priest's lips continued all the same, until they had to be stopped. Nothing ever really ceases until it has to stop. When the prisoner could stand it no longer, and he turned abruptly to stare down the priest. "Do you really believe all this nonsense about eternal hellfire?" he asked.

"Of course I believe it," replied the priest, caught off-guard at the condemned prisoner's candor. The prisoner condemned to die had no time left for futile arguments, but false piety demanded his snark.

"Well, I expect nothing but a serene, dreamless sleep." Who could have cared in the slightest whether a murderer believed in hell or grace? The prisoner continued, "But if I did believe in the hell you speak of, I would crawl from one coast of England to the other on hand and knee over broken glass if need be, and I would preach the gospel to the masses day and night without tiring if it meant saving even a single soul. That's what I would do if I believed in a God like yours."

Nothing changed. The prisoner was hanged. Perhaps Nietzsche put it best when he said the ability of an idea to comfort us is no guarantee of its truth. The prisoner never repented, and neither did the priest.[1]

---

1. Or perhaps he did. This story is loosely adapted from a likely apocryphal account of the execution of Charles Frederick Peace, who was executed for murder in 1879. Several historians paint a very different picture, wherein Peace converted to Christianity in prison and writes to everyone he knows about his newfound faith. The version I tell, where he is defiant and does not repent, has proliferated as a sermon illustration encouraging evangelism. The earliest version I have found of Peace's last words, defiant to the end, comes in 1905, which is odd, because the more evangelistically useful version of a story usually comes much later than the religiously disinterested historical account. My presumption is that Peace did repent, but I like the defiant sermon version more (even though I'm using it for exactly opposite reasons that preachers use the story). I am using this story not to suggest more evangelism but instead to suggest nobody truly believes in hellfire at an operative, day-to-day level. For the earliest defiant version of this story I've yet found, see the 1905 newspaper article by W. J. Dawson, "The Evangelism of Jesus."

2
Hypocrisy, Our Highest Virtue

A great Jewish rabbi named Abraham Joshua Heschel once said some-thing that has lurked in the background ever since: "*Intellectual honesty* is one of the supreme goals of philosophy of religion, just as self-deception is the chief source of corruption in religious thinking, more deadly than error. Hypocrisy rather than heresy is the cause of spiritual decay."[1] Here is how I learned what the sage meant.

I arrived at my vocation quite by accident, and I never had any ambi-tions to be a scholar or teacher. For most of my life, I assumed I would be a minister. I was raised in southern Evangelical territory, and I found both life and pain through it. A scholar I quite like, John D. Caputo, says my home is the land where God (of the Big Reductionistic Stories variety) will never die because the people do not dare think. Caputo cites my primary influence, the psychoanalyst Jacques Lacan, when he says, "Such religion is unbelievable. We don't believe it and there is no need to discredit it as it is making itself unbelievable all by itself, with every billboard it puts up attacking the theory of evolution, global warming, the emancipation of women and same sex marriage. With each passing day it makes itself more unbelievable with the 'dare not think' set, although, as Lacan points out, it will probably last forever in the Bible Belt (where they don't dare)."[2] The postmodern among us may reject the simple narrative, but for many the Big Reductionistic Story keeps an unsophisticated narrative in its place and prefers simple faith and so-called commonsense politics. Thinking is kept

1. Heschel, *God In Search of Man*, 10–11.
2. See Caputo, "Proclaiming the Year of Jubilee," 18.

to a limit, because rethinking triggers anxiety. A limit is something those in control use to define the boundaries of in-groups and out-groups, and this is particularly true of the world in which I grew up. It was during my time at university that reading began to fray the edges of my faith.

My Story

I'm no martyr, and I never thought crossing a single boundary would so dramatically change the course of my life. I was a pastor at a small church in the American south when my views on LGBT people began shifting away from the dogma I had inherited in childhood. I didn't even feel a need to hide my changing views, as the church had built itself around the idea that we should (at least, in theory) be open to different perspectives. As a member of the generation they call Millennials, I suspect my change of heart was no different than what so many of us from that culture went through. I simply had the complicating dimension of changing views while in a job that depends on never-changing views. It's been said the pastorate is the only profession in which professional development is discouraged.

I was summoned one morning for a meeting with the senior pastor where I was told my services where no longer welcome. My changing beliefs about gay friends and family were the purpose, and, to make my situation all the more certain, he numbered off other theological ideas on which I'd evolved. The flurry of accusations were bewildering to the point that, in all honesty, it would be months before I'd know for sure why I had been terminated. All I knew for sure was I had misjudged my position, and my world collapsed. But everything concealed will be unconcealed in time.

We've all felt the all-too-human need to find a course through the tempest. We have the sense there absolutely *must* be a coherent narrative to account for all the contradictions. Building a narrative takes time, and it requires a willingness to hear something new. One thing we will discuss in this book over and over again is how we continually return to old ideas and reinterpret them into new narratives. The events, facts, arguments, and texts are seldom what keep us up at night when compared against the sheer force of reinterpreting our stories for the worse. Any victim of trauma would tell you the same. After losing my job as a pastor, I spent nine months agonizing over what was wrong with me. The church world is a curious thing where differences of ideas can transform into accusations of character, and even childhood friends seemed supportive of my termination. I say this to tell you—as you've no doubt felt in your own life—I settled on a self-harming narrative through the tempest: I *must* be the one in the wrong, even if I couldn't see how.

The psychoanalysts rightly suggest we prefer to be ill. However much we consciously hate the feeling, we get unconscious pleasure from settling on a narrative where we are in the wrong. At least we can find a secured certainty when we decide we are wrong. We then unconsciously repeat behaviors and relationships that never work. When given the choice between the anxiety of unknowing and the certainty of defeat, we tend to fear anxiety so much that we take pleasure in our guilt.[3] It's true of me now, and it will be true of me in the future, but it was absolutely true of me for those nine months.

At the end of those nine months, I awoke to an email from one of the few, close friends who had supported me all along. The email advised I check the local news, where I learned my former pastor had been arrested for having a sexual relationship with an underage boy. I count it as one of the strangest days of mixed emotions I have ever experienced. There was sadness for his family and the church I had once helped lead. There was a sense of vindication as well—the type of vindication one hates oneself for feeling. What I felt strongest of all was what people often feel when they have been manipulated and so suddenly have the blinders ripped away: I felt as if I should keep my hurting and his arrest separate, as if the two had nothing to do with each other.

On the one hand, it's truly rare to be vindicated so clearly. On the other hand, nobody should feel happiness at the suffering of others. I asked myself this over and over again: what does it say about me if a family's darkest hour gave me any elation at all? In a sense, I wanted to keep thinking of myself as guilty, because it meant I had nothing to be happy about. We are such strange creatures, avoiding resolution while preferring guilt.

What became clear was that the pastor had used me as a form of denial. Ridding the community of my presence was an effective way for him to appear more safely conservative. Like many people who begin to rethink beliefs in a more fundamentalist setting, my self-judgment was sharp and honed. I had grown accustomed to hearing there was something erroneous with me ever since I began to rethink the traditional beliefs I grew up

---

3. Freud said this in several places, but my primary influence concerning anxiety throughout this book is Lacan, *Anxiety*.

with (a standard gaslighting tactic beloved by dogmatic types), but this was something altogether new. I couldn't help but wonder how my old friends who had sided against me would react after recognizing my termination was a small part of a criminal's cover story, but I had every confidence nobody would side with a convicted offender. I was a fool for thinking that.

Odd as it may sound, there is a sense in which a fundamentalist worldview sees progressive beliefs as *worse* than criminally abusive behavior. The former is often viewed as an active choice to desire evil, while the latter is often viewed as an accident of circumstance, a temporary failing, or some other cliché for which divine mercy exists. It's a curious worldview that actually sees a desire for equality as worse than assault. This could never be stated openly, for that would make the sham too obvious, but this logic hides inside the beast of organized religion.

I can't say what happened in the following months of discussion within that church, since I was no longer part of the community. I don't know how they came to understand those events, and I don't know if anyone ever made the link between their demand for conservative theological appearances and the duplicitous behavior of the pastor. I really don't know if anyone learned a thing. But here is one thing I can say: to this day, not one person ever apologized for participating in one of my darker moments. In fact, several old friends from that community actually became far more hostile towards me in the aftermath. Several still pastor churches which doubtlessly have no idea of their shepherd's capabilities to repress and lash out. Hostility is such an effective tool for covering over the need to rethink.

I share this story because it formed a kind of background for the work I do. For a long time it caused me anger, but I've come to appreciate it as a crucial lesson in human behavior. I study the differences between conscious ideas and unconscious behavior. When the two don't align, it's called hypocrisy. I'm only somewhat interested in the abstract theological ideas. I'm far more interested in (1) *how* certain beliefs function, how those beliefs create the identities we live into, and (2) *why* there is such a wide gulf between what we imagine we believe and what we unconsciously act as if we believe in our daily existence.

It's not the case that my former parishioners simply excused abuse. They were good people caught in the cunning and conceit of a charlatan. Then again, anxiety and repression make for a strangely predictable undependability. A community can forgive an abusive traditionalist faster than it can forgive a decent progressive thinker. I'm interested in why and how this happens. So let us keep the sage's words in our ears. "Hypocrisy rather than heresy is the cause of spiritual decay."[4]

Decay

It was a quote one finds thrown into the text in a way suggesting it never intended to be anything so profound, but the line haunted me ever after. Epiphanies never come when expected, nor are they found by regurgitating what we already know. They hide in new twist on stories we've heard so many times before. Epiphanies await in the parable we heard as a child, in the trauma we misrecognized, in the love we desire, and in the anger that needs a voice. We awaken to an idea that changes everything in retrospect, but we really can't blame ourselves for missing it before. We only arrive at the new by accident. Rather than choosing our beliefs, it seems our beliefs choose us.

One thing I believe with all my heart is this: hypocrisy is one of our most prized values. It is an unconscious value, so we don't see what lies before our eyes, but it is a high value nonetheless. This is all the more true for American Protestantism, and those of us who are theologians are under a constant threat. We lose our jobs when we teach what we know. Much of the public hasn't a clue about it, but it affects us all—the professor, the priest, the entrepreneur, the worker, and the parent.

We see it in our universities when those of us who teach are asked to sign those awful documents called statements of faith. The statements all read alike: do you *affirm* X, Y, and Z? We are asked to affirm, not believe, because actual belief is not the point. In a sense, it is not a matter of what we think we believe (in our innermost thoughts) or what we live as if we believe (in our concrete existence of everyday life); we are only expected to posture correctly. It's nearly a commandment: thou shalt bear false witness.

We see it in our popular culture too. I recently came across a truly ridiculous article asking why it is that American country music (which affiliates itself with generalized, white Evangelical values) celebrates living like hell on Saturday night and praying in the pews on Sunday morning. The article suggested it was hypocritical, which is only a conclusion we could draw if we thought the message on Sunday was actually meant to affect behavior.

4. Heschel, *God In Search of Man*, 10–11.

We see it in our political process, where those who think of themselves as pious exhibit the worst cruelties, who start wars and call torture "enhanced interrogation," and who cut aid to the most vulnerable, all while carrying on with secret affairs hidden from spouses. We call it hypocritical and quote a verse from their own Scriptures to prove the point. We do this because we think hypocrisy is something they'd desire to avoid. And surely enough, once we quote the verse we will hear a reply conjuring the limitless creativity we have for denying the obvious. We are told "don't judge," even though our supposed savior was quite clear with his feelings toward judging hypocrisy.

What are we guarding when we refuse to judge the harmful? Why refuse to designate the obvious before our eyes? For much of our religious culture, I'm arguing hypocrisy actually is the primary value, and admitting this allows us to think about a central theme in this book. When we encounter a claim which cannot possibly be true, the most important question we can ask is: (1) is this person an honest fool or (2) a cynic who simply does not care for the truth?

Didn't the Christ teach us how to deal with this question? When encountering the Pharisee, he knew hypocrisy reigned in the heart of his questioner. Sometimes the most ethical and direct way to deal with hypocrisy is to pretend as if the person truly believes what they say. "You blind guides!" he would say, "You strain out a gnat but swallow a camel."[5] There were Pharisees who foolishly believed every last word of their law and others who doubtlessly only acted the part, but the Christ acted as a jester pretending they believed every last word claimed. In so doing, he let their actions speak for themselves. It's an immense, historical irony that the most dogmatically religious types fail to see what their supposed savior thought of dogmatically religious types.

Another thing I believe without any doubt is this: the unconscious *will* speak. If we think of hypocrisy as a contradiction between our conscious self-perception and our unconscious reality, we should expect every contradiction to work its way to the surface in time. As the saying goes, the liar has to have a good memory. But when memory fails, the unconscious will speak, and our secrets will work their way to the surface. We can silence the contradictions for a while, but we cannot hide them forever. Beliefs can lie, but the anxiety behind them never lies. Those around us often know the

5. Matt 23:24 (NIV).

truth before we do. In the court of hypocrisy, the unconscious will demand a hearing.

In dealing with those doubts, we find the truth about ourselves. It's an honest question, really: do we seek the truth however we find it, or would we rather persist with the same views we've always had? We begin to ask questions hoping we'll gain answers to the ever-growing list of questions, and then we come to realize many of our questions were a farce. As any parent knows, maturity naturally needs a great deal of immaturity to come first, for we only become mature through the process of trial and error.

Consider the way this works with so many sincerely pious people who hold the same beliefs they held as teenagers. They haven't changed views since their parents first implanted those views in them as children. Sincerely pious people will protest loudly that their faith is true, and they will mean it from the depths of their soul. But maturity is, again, a long process, and if there is no change then there is no maturity. Their protests claiming they have the Truth is as loud as the anxiety they hold in check.

Once again, orthodoxy is what we cling to whenever we fear thinking about the doctrine itself. It's easy to cling to orthodoxies and dogmas and Truths (always with a capital T), but it's much more difficult to open ourselves to rethinking what we hold dearest. Thusly so, questions lead to more questions that beget uncontrollable doubts. We might foster or repress our doubts—this is certainly happening all around us at every moment—but in the end our beliefs choose us rather than the other way around. You read this book or that, but the very act of answer-seeking already tells you a flood approaches.

There used to be miracle workers who traveled from village to village healing the tribesmen of every ill. Aches and pains and barrenness and demon possession. Then someone invented the sciences, another invented medicines, another invented books, another invented gods, another invented laws, and we became fragmented. Our thoughts were spread across disciplines, and no man or woman could hold all the knowledge in one mind anymore. We gained some knowledge, but we couldn't know everything any longer. So we conjured the fiction of an all-knowing leader, perhaps a charlatan. We used to do this with shamans, and we do it today with the priest and the pundit. Life is easier if we can simply pay a hypocrite for advice.

Those who claim to have the Truth, those who admit no doubt, are always a fool or cynic (and usually the latter). They convince us with their confidence, for we have a curious tendency to give our trust to those who claim they know. If the charlatan isn't a complete fool, then he will have all the same doubts we hold close. But he will not say it. He makes his living by posturing, by affirming, and (without us realizing it) telling us everything we already think is perfectly right. He can contribute literally nothing yet get paid and revered all the same.

Just as hunger pangs arise and subside, the desire for learning either becomes satiated and complacent or instead an addictive craving. An addiction for learning afflicts very few people. And if it is true a pound of learning is not worth an ounce of youth, it is difficult not to envy those who would rather not know.

Here is a third thing I belief deeply: we never entirely *suppress* our desires or ideas. They are never purged out of existence, but instead we only clear them out from view. Whatever we falsely think we've suppressed will continue to haunt us in the background.

You Know, but Does the Big Other Know?

There a was girl who was the perfect child, if such a person even exists. In all she did, she strived toward the proud approval of her parents who told her what to desire. She was a rare case of being raised with the clarity that everything she did lied upon the right path. She was praised for her kindness, she was a team player, and she was the center of every social circle. She dated the right people, went on to the right schools, began her career at the right firm, married the right person, and began a family of her own with all the unconditional love her parents gave her. If there ever was someone who had everything she desired, it was her.

The world stopped on the day she received the tragic phone call. Her parents had been traveling along a small road late one night. The other driver never imagined his choice along the road that evening would bring an end to her paradise, but her life would never be the same after the loss of her parents.

She was catatonic with sorrow for months. Her friends and family members rallied around her, but nothing could bring her back. Her marriage suffered, and her life closed in on itself. Her nights were haunted by terrifying dreams. It was really only one nightmare—of her parents' last thoughts before then end—but their final words were always etched away by the image of collision.

As her condition deteriorated, her remaining family and friends pressed her, pleading, "You know the nightmare will not end, don't you? Pain doesn't end on its own." She resisted until she did not. We always repeat and resist until we cannot. So after many months of urging—after her relationships were falling apart, after her job was at risk, and after her habits became addictions—she entered the psychoanalyst's office one day.

She told the analyst of the great many things leading to this point. She told of her parents' tragic death, of her fears about her strained marriage, and she even confessed she no longer wished to be a mother at all. She eventually told the analyst she'd prefer to die as well. She told the analyst every last detail with the exception of one. We hide our story among other stories, and we hope we will not be discovered.

"You have told me a great deal of your traumas," the veteran analyst countered, "but you've said nothing about your nightmares."

In a desperate shock that only ever comes when we do not want to face ourselves, she fired back, "You haven't listened to a word I've said!"

"Indeed, I've tried not to hear your justifications, but I've gathered enough. You must be haunted, yes?—'are they proud of me?,' or 'are they looking down from Heaven and proud of me?,' or maybe even 'were they thinking of me in their last moment?'"

"You act as if I don't know my parents are gone!" she countered, so very angry at the analyst who refused to hear her words.

"No, I'm quite sure you know there is no big Other commanding your life any longer, though you deeply wish there was. You are here because you absolutely *do* know your parents are dead." And the analyst paused, unsure of whether she had ears to hear. "But do your parents know?"

3 The Replacement and the Placeholder

If we want to talk about theology, then we have to talk about what language does. Words don't simply communicate the world as it is; rather, words actively construct what we expect to find. We talk ourselves into an ideal version of ourselves. The philosopher Ludwig Wittgenstein said that, instead of thinking of language simply as words referring to ideas, we should think of language as a kind of game. A game is impossible to play when new rules are invented halfway through the game. This of course is crucial for us to understand in a book about cynics and fools, for the actual *intent* of our language (is it a tool for power, or merely a means for communication?) is at least as important as the content. We can explore this concept of language games through the popular board game Risk. In the game, players attempt to build armies and capture territories across an archaic map. A player wins the game once she has vanquished all opposing armies and captured the world for herself, so any player can strike any other at any time.

Anyone who has played Risk will likely have experienced the request for alliances; one player will ask another to agree not to attack for a round or two with the assumption alliance will work out well for both. All the other players will likely sigh in frustration, because the conjured alliance means more armies can be reallocated at previously ill-defended borders. Alliances are common in such games, but they change the dynamics of the game precisely because they effectively (if only temporarily) change the rules of the game. Or more precisely, an alliance changes expectations of what a player will do. All of our language is like this. We have one set of expectations surrounding meaning, but another person will mean a very different set of things through those same words. So in this chapter and the next, we are going to interrogate the games of our words and thoughts. What happens when you and I use all the same words, ideas, and dogmas, but we mean something completely different?

Repression Covers the Void

In the story of the girl and her parents, I used the term *big Other*. It's a term from psychoanalysis, but it doesn't simply mean gods or parents, friends or cultures, religions or political ideologies. The big Other might well manifest as any of these things, but it is first and foremost a position in the mind that must be filled. When I ask myself if I am happy in a relationship, I might ask whether my partner is happy. When I ask if I am guilty, I might ask whether God or Law is satisfied with my actions. When I want to know my opinions are correct, I seek out authorities who will verify what I want to have verified. We desire, we act, and we know all in relation to an imagined big Other. We imagine the big Other is out there, but it's in our heads. The girl in my story consciously knew her parents were dead, but her parents (representing the big Other) didn't know; the version of them in her head was still directing her anxieties, desires, and depression. The big Other might not exist, but it can still drive everything we do.

Here is another game having everything to do with the loss of the big Other, and it comes from the psychoanalyst Sigmund Freud.[1] The story investigates the impossibility of *suppressing* anxieties. We *repress* rather than suppress, and there is a world of difference. Suppression stamps out a fire; repression simply keeps the fire out of mind while it burns in the background. The police can suppress protests, but physical suppression can be a way of further repressing the deeper causes of the protest (racism, economic disenfranchisement). The mechanisms of suppression are easy to see, and while religion might excel at suppressing certain behaviors, it cannot keep the repressed anxieties from returning with a vengeance. Whatever is repressed will always return in disguise.

Freud's grandson had a habit of inventing new games for entertainment. Is a game simply entertainment, or is it possible the game is doing something beyond mere entertainment? One day, the child cobbled together a simple toy out of a cotton reel and a piece of string. The boy would hold

1. Freud, "Beyond the Pleasure Principle," 599–601

the string in one hand and cast the toy over the edge of his crib and shout *fort!* (the German word for "gone"). After the toy was out of sight under the crib, he would yank back on the string, pulling the reel back up into the crib while shouting *da!* ("there"). Over and over again, the infant played this incessant game of *fort* and *da, fort* and *da, fort* and *da*. Occasionally infants act like adults, or perhaps it is the other way around.

The young boy only ever entertained himself with this game when his mother was out of sight. The worst versions of a hasty psychoanalysis (making for a tightly wrapped story) might imagine the infant was using the cotton reel as a simple *replacement* for the absent mother. This hasty judgement is exactly the misstep of every religious apologetic.[2] Surely, sometimes we engage in a ritual that simply matches up as a replacement for something missing, but this case isn't all too interesting to me. What's interesting is the infant was perfectly well aware the mother was gone, but the game provided security all the same.

What if our ridiculous games aren't a replacement for what we cannot have but instead a *placeholder* for what couldn't be replaced? The boy engaged in this game when the mother was out of the room, and it kept him happy for the moment, but he was under no illusion that a cotton reel replaced his mother. It was a representative-in-the-place-of-a-representation, a placeholder instead of a replacement. Likewise, might everything we hold closely on a leap of faith—our desires, our gods, and our demons—all serve a much more basic purpose of covering over a void we cannot bear to acknowledge beneath us?

Let's push further. The boy in this story (1) desired comfort, nourishment, and security (which was normally supplied by the mother), but he also (2) desired all those things even in the mother's absence. Thus the mother became the idealized fixation of comfort in his young imagination. But when deprived of what he idealized (during the mother's absence), he needed to cover over her absence with a stand-in object (the cotton reel toy). We call this process repression rather than suppression. What I mean by repression is this: when we can't have two things we desire at the same time, the desire for one must be pushed down (put out of our awareness, or made unconscious). The boy's desire for comfort outweighed his desire for the mother herself, so he put her absence out of mind and into the void of

2. By religious apologetics, I'm referring to the crafty arguments we use to defend problematic beliefs. Of course, we only feel the need to defend those beliefs because we do in fact sense they are problematic. Since we enjoy repeating what doesn't work, we repress our suspicions and persist with ideas that don't work.

the unconscious. He did this with the simplest toy. However, if Freud had snatched the toy away from the young boy, he would have experienced the full horror of the absent mother.

When I was a child, I treasured a cheap compass gifted to me by a relative one Christmas. The relative was a distant uncle who I only saw once a year on Christmas Eve, and when he passed away it was not a very traumatic moment for my young self. However, when I realized I had lost the compass some months later, I was inconsolably upset with the feeling I had lost my last connection to the uncle. It was not when he passed away but instead when I lost the toy that I actually experienced the loss. The compass was repressing loss, and the loss of the compass became the loss of the uncle.

Whatever is unconscious is in the driver's seat. The boy's *fort-da* game was, in a sense, being directed by the very thing he wanted to keep out of mind. Rather than suppressing altogether (to the extent the denied idea no longer affects us), we always repress: we push down, we keep out of sight, and we let our ideas float in the unconscious background. But it does not work, and this is a book about ideas that do not work. What is repressed will return as something else. The repressed and the *return of the repressed* are one and the same. Whatever is repressed will continue to inflict itself, but it will inflict in disguise. We might repress depression with alcohol, loneliness with bad relationships, boredom with faith, and anger with self-righteousness, but the repressed will always return in an inverted and disguised form. All of our waking thoughts are not so different from an child entertaining himself with a simple game.

Other games with the big Other don't turn out so well. The story of the fall of Adam and Eve in Genesis works in exactly the same way as this *fort-da* game. The fall is supposedly where the primordial couple first experimented with sin by eating fruit at a serpent's behest, but another way of reading the story suggests it was the beginning of civilization. We created rules in the aftermath of sin, and we guard rules with ever-expanding rules. The repressing placeholder (whether a toy or a doctrine) becomes guarded with other objects and ideas. Because our games hide whatever we repress, our innocuous rules become guarded with more and more rules which must be defended as well. To question one part of the game is felt as an attack on the entire game, so we unconsciously start to make connections to other objects, beliefs, or desires that can't be questioned either. We'll return to the story of the fall later, but let's take note: God never tells Eve not to touch the tree. Nevertheless, when the serpent asks Eve if it was true she mustn't eat of the tree, she expanded the prohibition—not only must she never eat the fruit, but she decided she must also avoid touching the tree entirely.

Once the taboo is established, the rule expands outward and invents new taboos. Whether a taboo behavior or a taboo idea, the first prohibition quickly leads to a second, a third, and so on. After guarding our idols with so many rules, we cease to wonder why we worshiped the idol in the first place. You have felt this when you lost Belief X, and before you knew it there was a cascade of lost belief. The flood began with a drop of rain.

Maturity Reads Mistakes

Maturity is learning, and learning is rethinking. Some are content to keep all the same ideas they held as Truth when they were five or fifteen years old. Repetition of the old is simply easier, and just as our bodies seek homeostasis, our minds prefer mental stasis. Somewhere along the line, someone advised me to always try reading above my current reading level. The idea is simple: if I try to read material more difficult than I'm able to understand now, I'll be able to master more sophisticated material soon enough. This is how I learned to read.

Early in my seminary studies, I came to a point where the theological questions I began with no longer had the same importance. They weren't the questions that seemed to matter anymore. I wanted to know what the great thinkers said about the big philosophical questions, and I ended up wondering how many of the big questions were just covering up even bigger anxieties. Did the expert have an answer? Did the teacher rise to fame only to regret having nobody left to ask? Does any theologian ever mean what they say? Is every idea just a game getting perpetually reworked in real time?

For me, the answer came from one of those moments we never expected to be profound. Maybe it was only a half-answer, because the truth can only ever be said in halves, *en route* toward an answer. We start studying theology with the assumption that we know what the field entails, for the Greek etymology of the word *theology* indeed suggests it is a word about God. But in short order, we theologians find ourselves studying so many cognate fields—history, philosophy, critical theories, politics, economics, anthropology, and so on—that we never expected to engage.

Early in my studies, I was at a large conference of religion scholars in San Francisco. A friend and I were standing on an escalator delivering us to the next session as I lamented, "Does this theologian ever really mean what she writes? She's brilliant, but she never finally spells out the metaphor."

My friend was a step or two above me on the escalator, the effect being that a brilliant mind was augmented by the additional dimension of literally looking down at me, a young novice trying to make sense of philosophy and theology. He said something that stuck with me: "There are theologians who say *what* they mean, and there are theologians who say *at* what they mean—one isn't necessarily better than the other, but you have to know which type you are dealing with."[3]

To say something worth hearing takes different routes, and sometimes saying *at* what we mean is the only way to say anything at all. To speak *at* is an indirect method that points in a direction but never spells it out plainly. It's often frustrating to read indirect theory, but sometimes this is the only way to speak of matters too complex or contested for direct confrontation. Sometimes a battle can only be won by attacking the flanks rather than confronting the opponent head on, and the battle of ideas works the same. To speak indirectly lets the reader gather more conclusions than the author could ever propose. My friend's answer changed the way I read books, and I want to be very clear that I am the latter; I say *at* what I mean. We read our own perspectives and experiences into books. Just as we shape our gods after ourselves, we shape our readings after our own likeness. I will say a few things with great specificity, but more often I will beg you to twist my meaning and make it yours.

A twisted or misunderstood meaning is the risk of every parable, the edge to every joke, the pitfall of every life's work, and the ground of meaning-making. To be cryptic enough to bear meaning will also be cryptic enough to be misunderstood. Every great teacher knows this. I don't intend to tell you much, at least not much of what to think. My goal is to suggest a method of how to interrogate.

Of course, the strategy of speaking *at* or toward something only works if there is more going on inside theology than we see at first, for it is entirely possible you misinterpret me or I misinterpret the world. We are on this journey of the big questions together, and none of us gets out of here alive. The early theologian Saint Augustine wrote that humankind listens to poets

---

3. I should thank Tripp Fuller for changing the way I read theory with this brief conversation.

rather than scientists. The downside, as he rightly pointed out, is that nothing is more loquacious than folly. Both the fool and the philosopher alike have many, many words. I want you to think of this book as an adventure of ideas probing *how* our beliefs hold us. The *what* to believe can be sorted out on your own.

When Rabbi Heschel wrote of hypocrisy and heresy in a book called *God In Search of Man*, the title already hinted of speaking indirectly at something. A God doesn't need to search for long to find us, but we are so very skilled at hiding from our gods and demons. Rabbi Heschel said we who do the work of theology and philosophy have a paramount responsibility for intellectual honesty. Honesty is the supreme goal, just as deception is the source of corruption. We needn't worry our ideas are heresies, for all of our ideas are always a type of *false consciousness,* a perception of the world rooted in conditions of class, economy, and so many forces beyond our control or awareness. Our ideas are a game with ever-changing rules, a way of interpreting a world that must be interpreted. What rots the soul is not the false consciousness (thinking the wrong thing) but the conflicts wrought by our hypocrisy. As the psychoanalyst Carl Jung once said: summoned or not, the gods will come. I prefer to speak indirectly as well.

Many popular theologians like to imagine there are certain beliefs that are negotiable while others are non-negotiable. Whoever decided on such a ridiculously small view of the world was clearly a genius, for he convinced the masses to think the options were as simple as this or that. If I were to ask you, "Select either this idea or it's opposite; which will it be?" then one thing is clear: you never had much of a choice. If we receive an answer that we were already expecting, was it really a question?[4]

4. I'm paraphrasing Lacan, who asked, "If we receive the answer we were expecting, is it really an answer?" Lacan, *The Ego In Freud's Theory and in the Technique of Psychoanalysis*, 237.

Noah and His God

Noah was never quite the same after the great flood. He couldn't tell his family of his feelings of treachery, or how badly he wished he could have been swallowed by the waters. There was only loneliness now, and only a ration of wine left over from the better times to ease the pain.

He was praised by his family as the savior of humankind. It was his own doing really, so easy it is to reframe our misdeeds in pious words. He told himself he was a good person, but the screams of innocent children in the water still haunted his dreams. Piety and wine solved most of his troubles, though he hadn't much needed gods before the great flood. The dual addictions kept his great betrayal out of mind. It worked until it didn't work, and when it didn't work he would ask himself, "Who strikes a deal to save only his family? And with what devil did I strike the deal?"

The question was only occasional, for he hadn't many close ties in the previous epoch. Escaping judgment with only his cohort was an easy enough decision when nobody he loved was going to perish. Of course, that was then, before he had gained the world but lost his own soul's ability to love anything. "Mocking my warnings all those years we were building," he figured, "they had their chances to apologize, those poor and foolish wretches."

He had never before felt such ecstatic joy as he did on the day the floodgates of judgment rained down upon the earth. Perhaps his joy at rain had been a peculiar place to judge the world, but this couldn't cross his mind, so powerful were his addictions to dull his faculties.

The cries of the drowning still haunted his dreams here in his new paradise. "What a godforsaken night it was when the first rains came," was what he would have said if he could have felt the brutality of the hellish deal he cut for an exit. What kind of man makes that bargain? If not for knowing his alcohol would forgive him, he wouldn't have been able to bear it. The god of wine was his lonely company now, a figment of imaginative illusion, a flight from the troubles, and an expert in justifying the desire for revenge.[1]

1. This story was partly inspired by Berrigan, *A Book of Parables*.

4 Saints are Empty Signifiers

Here is a lesson I learned about saints: they are a blank canvas upon which we paint our imagination. No matter how theist or atheist, no matter how traditional or progressive, we have a peculiar tendency to think our saints would agree with us (often on every single issue). Whether the figure is Martin Luther King Jr., Aristotle, or Christ, we turn them into version who thought like us. I was standing just outside the old Supreme Court chamber during my first trip to Washington, DC, when I learned how saints are a canvas for our imagination.

My friend was a staffer working in the congressional office building next to the capitol. There is an underground tunnel they take from one building to the other. We descended through the man-made cavern and reached the bowels of the capitol. Before the Supreme Court had its own building, it met in a dark, cold room in the capitol's basement level. My mind turned into a swirling mix of history and the ominous feeling one naturally has when thinking on so many good and horrific decisions made in the room so long ago.

Outside the room, there was a dark grey statue. My guide asked if I could identify the man. "I haven't seen this one before," I told him. He smiled, hinting I was caught in a tour-standard gimmick and was about to feel had. I could not place the character even as I quickly played a list of names and faces my mind had collected from years of history books. "I promise you've seen this one before," he told me. I gave up and asked for the answer.

To be sure, the only similarity between that statue and the George Washington in my textbooks was the absence of his 318 slaves. The statue's features were those of an elderly man, coarse and hunched, and there was nothing statesmanlike about him at all. My friend explained how the statue was one of the first representations made of him. When we don't have a precise date for a work of art, we compare it to other depictions with known dates. Historians gauge this work as one of the earliest, because there was an artistic difference in Washington's depiction starting about ten years after his death. His features became smoothed over with an eternal youthfulness, his gestures became elegant and pronounced, and often enough there is something like a heavenly halo encircling the primordial father's head. He became a saint, and one must always *misremember* a saint.

How to Misremember

I have the memory of this tour tucked away, for it taught me something about the saints being empty signifiers. The tour happened only weeks before I began my seminary studies, which is where I learned about other misremembered stories of men with halos around their heads.

I remember this story every year on the day commemorating Martin Luther King Jr., for he is another who must be misremembered. I see my conservative friends praising a religious leader who dreamed of a "color-blind" society. I see my liberal friends remembering a man who decried warfare and the selectively brutal fist of racism entrenched in our laws. I see very few remembering a man who was so radical he even considered the white liberal an obstacle.[1] I see very few remembering a man who had no tolerance for those who think both sides have a point. I see very few remembering a man for whom the traditional *status quo* was nothing other than white supremacy with a smile. I see very few remembering his economic views or proposals on poverty, his anti-militarism which could never be tolerated in American society today, and his loud rage against the powers that be. It's been said King fell to the assassin's bullet at the last possible moment, for his increasing radicalism would soon have made him reviled in the same way many reviled Malcolm X.

The latter, Malcolm X, is *not* misremembered; his story is often denied from the history books altogether, for those who write histories with happy

---

1. The criticism of the progressive yet hesitant white moderate is something everyone should read in Martin Luther King Jr.'s "Letter from a Birmingham Jail."

endings did not deem him worthy of existence. King fell early enough to be co-opted by those who prefer to misremember. He became a hero to the oppressed and oppressor alike, for oppressors can remember the version they prefer. The saint is a mantle to take up and wear like a jersey for our arbitrary teams, and those in power don't really mind our misremembering. In fact, the powerful depend on our misremembering.

I began my seminary studies with this lesson on misremembering, and I found its infection in each new idea we explored in theology courses. We would study saints, patriarchs, matriarchs, mystics, and prophets, and we came face-to-face with our assumptions they would view us the same way we viewed them: simple, consistent, and right. Of course, no two people ever view everything in the same way. Should I ask you everything you think about Idea X, there is not a single person in the world who would perfectly match your answers. We say "Let's compare what this one person says to the same Greek word in another book," as if two authors ever mean the exact same thing. We paint our Scriptures like a blank canvas (or more precisely, we paint over the picture already there). When we read a prophet, we tend to assume he or she held all the same views as every other. And those prophets, who surely must all agree with each other on everything, also must agree with us. We assure ourselves that our intentions are humility. We guard ourselves with fanciful terms like hermeneutics or inerrancy, all for the goal of Truth. Actually, we should've called it narcissism.

We are narcissists beholden to our affiliations (this team or that, this nation or that, this faith or that). The New Testament tells us we are supposedly neither Jew nor Gentile, neither male nor female, and neither slave nor free.[2] Those categories were not arbitrary. The apostle was cutting across three key points for identity in the ancient world. The ancient world wasn't all that different from today. We are put in our places, and we didn't get a vote.

Encoding Our Narcissism

We have an ethnicity. We are assigned a gender. We are given social and economic circumstances. We are told these are important, fixed, and unquestionable. In the modern world we are told we may make of ourselves what we like and "pull ourselves up by our bootstraps," but the force of circumstance ensures we shall not travel far from our so-called rightful place.

2. See Gal 3:28.

After all, we don't actually live in a meritocracy where our efforts are fairly rewarded, do we? No, instead we tend toward defining ourselves by the jobs we do, the friends we keep, the hobbies with which we distract ourselves. We are thrown into the world and latch onto certain points for identity, but we only have so many options. We do not choose between poverty and wealth so much as it is almost always chosen for us. Our beliefs are much the same.

But what is Paul trying to say in this peculiar verse? If he is denying the facts of the world, then he is a fool. If he is conning us into an alternate version of reality (a bait and switch of souls), then he is a cynic. Are we not ethnic, gendered, transactional beings? Perhaps, but if we give the apostle the benefit of a doubt and see something inspired in this text, maybe we see a counterintuitive move away from Truth (of the kind never doubted) and toward truths (which we are always in the process of learning).

Consider it this way: the master has everything to lose if he loses his slave, while the slave has nothing to lose (and everything to gain) with the loss of the master.[3] In the early Christian communities, a master and slave would gather together at the same table and, in theory, obey Paul's command to lay their identities aside while the bread and wine were passed. Of course, the catch is we never lay down our identities for long. At the close of those meetings, it became perfectly clear again who was lord and who was bondsman. And the existence of a slave is the truth of that church.

The slave is a symptom of a deeply oppressive economy. Perhaps when the apostle says we are neither slave nor free, he effectively means, "You hold slaves?!" Who we harm defines our character in a way no other identity marker could. Was Paul cryptic enough to be meaningful, or, put differently, was he cryptic enough to be misremembered and misunderstood?

Thinking about oppression is not only important for dismantling oppression. Thinking about oppression also shows us how ideology blinds us to the truth before our eyes. Examining misunderstandings is a way to understand ourselves. When I teach my students the history of Christianity, one of our most difficult topics examines how nineteenth-century Christians justified slavery. Preachers and theologians claimed slavery was supported by the Bible in Levitical rules for slaveholding, the curse on Noah's son Ham (who left going south into Canaan or perhaps Africa), or the fact Paul sent an escaped slave back to his master. The Christian

---

3. I am referencing the dialectic of lord and bondsman in Hegel, *Phenomenology of Spirit*. I will return to this idea in the final chapter.

slave apologists made practical arguments about the role of cotton in the Southern economy. They made dubious appeals to Christian charity and claimed slavery was the only way to make sure slaves were taught Christian principles. They said questioning the biblical view in favor of slavery would take the slippery slope to atheism or socialism.[4]

Almost all of those arguments began with acknowledging the awfulness of slavery. Almost all of them included a section where they said they personally know many slaves who are happy slavery exists. I read these demeaning arguments, and I watch as my students recognize all the same arguments we see today. I hear them laugh when I read a quote from one Baptist pastor who recommended cutting ties with seditious people who advocate abolition.

There is a famous anarchist quote claiming: "The only church that illuminates is a burning church!"[5] The source was right in ways beyond its intention. What was meant as a cynical cut against the institution takes on a new life today; often enough, burning down our traditions is the only way forward. But there is another meaning in it as well connected to the apostle's claim that we are neither slave nor free.

In America, the image of the burning church means something a European writer couldn't understand, for in America we have a history of setting African American churches ablaze. We have a centuries-long history of racial hatred, and we have an equally long history of denying this centuries-long history. We call ourselves color blind, which is our way of telling those who are harmed that their views do not matter. But just as the truth of the lord is that he owns slaves, the truth of American liberty is the oppression of people for their skin. The truth of a white supremacist yet supposedly color-blind society is that those who protest injustice are called seditious.

We've recently seen an example of this color-blind protest—which signals something we'd rather not know—with the All Lives Matter counter to the Black Lives Matter movement. As a common analogy goes, in same way cries to save the rainforest do not imply we should burn all other kinds of forests, Black Lives Matter means exactly what it says. The movement

4. Yes, the slippery slope argument is nothing new. A slippery slope argument is what we deploy when our argument can't stand on its own feet, so we invent alternate realities. The Presbyterian theologian James Henley Thornwell argued that if the abolitionists got their way, it would end in a world of atheism, socialism, or communism in his essay "The Rights and Duties of Masters."

5. This quote, misattributed to Buenaventura Durruti, and its explanation, can be found in Žižek, "Dialectical Clarity Versus the Misty Conceit of Paradox," 287.

isolates a particular problem, namely, the killing of unarmed black persons, and it says black lives should matter as much as any others. So many people of my skin color heard this cry for equality as a demand for special treatment. Further, though detractors say we should not privilege one race over another (as they misinterpret Black Lives Matter activists to be doing), they usually feel no indignation over particular support for police or military personnel. Misinterpretation tells us something. Controversy always signals something repressed, and All Lives Matter is a return of the repressed. When calls for justice or a more egalitarian society yield such aggressive counteracting protests, we know a nerve has been touched—we know there is something happening that society wishes to keep not knowing. We'll conjure every argument to say it isn't so.

Fear sustains the pain. It's been said the greatest irony of oppression today, in all its forms, is that the very same people who stand to gain the most will fight the hardest to remain servile.[6] As the philosophers Gilles Deleuze and Félix Guattari wrote, "The fundamental problem of political philosophy is still precisely . . . 'Why do men fight *for* their servitude as stubbornly as though it were their salvation?'" We see this when middle-class men fight against higher pay for themselves. We see this when nearly everyone in society considers themselves middle class and yet claims that we haven't a class system. We see this when women consider it right that they are subservient according to patriarchal social values. We see this when mothers and fathers love their gay children yet protest their child's right to marry whomever they love. We see this in the very myth of a meritocracy—where we sincerely believe hard work will reap a reward, and then go about our day complaining of how we don't get the recognition we deserve.

We have these contradictions all around us, and they remind us of this very simple observation from the Apostle Paul. Yes, it would be ideal to live and gather together as if we were neither slave nor free, neither male nor female, neither Jew nor Gentile, neither North American nor Middle Eastern, neither white nor black, neither Republican nor Democrat, neither rich nor poor. Indeed it would be the best of all possible futures, but so long as there are contradictions between us, we had best listen to the messages of the contradictions. Further, we must listen to those excluded by the society we construct. This is the only path toward humility, for only the supremely arrogant believes they have nothing to learn from the excluded other.

6. Deleuze and Guattari, *Anti-Oedipus*, 29.

The philosophers have a name for this rethinking of names. The Apostle Paul gave us a short list of names (slave and free, male and female, Jew and Gentile), and then he called those names into question. He didn't spell out the implications, but instead he left it to us to think on how far those binary names should go. He was writing *at* something without telling us what. It's easy to imagine a faithful person affirming such a short list, and it is just as easy to imagine how shocked the same person would be if the list where expanded to include "neither Christian nor atheist." It's a legitimate question: how far down the path of questioning names should we go?

What's In a Name? Deconstructing Signifiers and Master Signifiers

The philosophers call these names *signifiers*. A signifier is a symptom of culture. The signifier tells us who we are, what vocations we should entertain, what views to hold, and what clothes to wear. Signifiers are handed to us on a media platter, taught in our schools, disciplined by our parents, and reinforced by our friends. Signifiers are the names we adopt—son, friend, faithful, introverted—to give ourselves a story. This brings up the matter of ranking signifiers.

If certain signifiers are more important (such as how being a parent is more important than being a fan of this or that sport), then is there such thing as a Master Signifier? Do certain signifiers outrank and organize all the rest? More importantly, would we even be able to recognize it as a Master Signifier?

I write this during the turmoil called political campaign season, and recently this exact question came up. A presidential candidate said he was a Christian first and an American second. Many voters had no problem with this, while the more secular found it outrageous. If the message of Christianity is true, then it's only consistent to say it should be the Master Signifier, the Truth beyond all other truths.

One catch is the candidate also calls himself a close follower of the Constitution, and the Establishment Clause of the First Amendment suggests there can be no national religion. Can someone who says Christianity outweighs everything else also, while in office, treat Christianity as only one religion among others? Clearly the answer in practice is yes, but it is not completely clear whether the answer can be logically consistent. If a candidate were Muslim and called himself a Muslim first and an American second, it's not much of a secret what the resulting popular reaction would be.

Christianity has a privileged status in America, which clearly gives the Christian candidate a lot of leeway. His or her beliefs are not scrutinized the way someone of another (or no) faith would be scrutinized. A Christian is not suspected of terrorism at the airport, and a Christian is rarely suspected of indoctrinating children at the schools. A Christian is not criticized for living according to the laws of her religion, and neither is she accused of having no values (regardless of how she actually lives). A Christian has an advantage in society, because Christianity is normal in a society where more than seven in ten profess this faith. But does this mean Christianity is what the philosophers (not to mention candidates and leaders) might call a Master Signifier? Not quite, but it floats into usage whenever expedient.

Every signifier points toward another signifier. Religions don't actually work as a Master Signifier but instead conceal (as a placeholder) a Master Signifier. Consider a dictionary as an example. The book is filled with words, each of which point to other words. There isn't a singular word defining all the other words in the dictionary, but instead each word refers to another. We only understand one word through the context of other words. If we could play on the idea of the Truth (the all-knowing perspective) and little truths (facts), perhaps we could say there is no Word in the dictionary; there are only words. If we say there is not one final Word, it wouldn't mean we have done away with words and language. We would only mean we don't have the God's-eye view. It's a position of humility.

In an Eastern creation myth the world is balanced upon the back of a giant turtle. What then, we ask, is the turtle balanced upon? The sage must reply with the only answer providing any sense—another turtle. We have a peculiar need to find solid ground at the bottom of everything. Perhaps instead it's just turtles all the way down.

Here is another example of what I mean by Truth and truths, Word and words, or Master Signifier and signifiers. When I say "I'm putting my glass on the table," it doesn't matter that at the subatomic level the electrons in the cup are repelled by the electrons on the table's surface. The facts of physics are simple enough; at the subatomic level, there isn't actually any physical contact. Instead, there's only a contact between electrical fields. But we don't seem to care, and we'd certainly grow annoyed with anyone who felt it extremely important to correctly state, "I'm only appearing to put my glass on the table, but actually particle physics tells us there is a fraction of space between the two." We don't speak like this, because in normal language it only seems to matter that our meaning gets close enough. Gods and glasses are not so different, and to insist our words are the final Word is a haughty hubris.

Theology should learn this lesson against hubris. The philosophers also have a name for the other path of humility, and they call it *deconstruction*. The philosopher Jacques Derrida explained it this way: every law aims at justice, but every law falls short of justice.[7] No rule—from the provincial speed limit to the national constitution—captures justice with perfection. If we suddenly think a rule is the perfect Rule, or that any law is the final measure of Justice, then we have made an idol out of a human rule. People who love laws usually don't see the contradiction with their recitations about being free from the law. There are those who love rules so much they'd gladly give their lives to the service of rules—they are generally those who merely give lip service to freedom from law.

If there is a difference between the existing law and the ideal of Justice, it led Derrida to say that we must always be midstream in deconstruction. He didn't mean destruction outright but rather deconstructing whatever is less than the ideal. We must always be rethinking our ideas and examining them from every side, for no idea is the final Idea. Perhaps there is a final Word, Idea, or Truth out there, but we haven't the access to it. We are flesh and blood struggling to make our world better, and we must bravely take the more difficult (and only humble) route through rethinking everything we were handed: our beliefs, our constitutions, our roles and vocations, our books, and every corner of every ideology.

Ideologies tell us to submit, and the great irony of thinking beings is that we do tend to fight for our servitude. There are all sorts of words, ideas, relationships, debts, and affiliations to designate who we are and to what tribe we affiliate. The first signifiers are handed to us by our parents. In adolescence they expand to schools and friends and teams and hobbies. In early adulthood they expand to politics and books and faith. Signifiers define us as American, vegan, married, blue collar, faithful, queer, or atheist. Each new word cordons off a part of us. A claim is made upon a part of our world. We create our beliefs, and our beliefs create us right back.

---

7. The idea of deconstructing laws in order to reach toward an undeconstructible ideal of justice was the subject of the first philosophical article I ever read. It changed the way I see words, doctrines, and laws forever. See Derrida, "Force of Law."

In the previous example of the political candidate who called himself a Christian first and an American second, I want to argue he was unwittingly (or perhaps intentionally and cynically) trying to fit in with how he imagined his voters would describe him. He was clearly trying to make a statement on his priorities, but his real goal was to communicate "I'm just like you!" (or perhaps "You are just like me!"). He used the names of Christian and American not to tell us what ultimately defines him but rather as placeholders concealing what actually defines him.

As the Apostle Paul taught us, we were given a place and a range of things we are allowed to believe. So long as we stay inside our boxes—our ethnic, gendered, and social boxes—the system can flex to accept any variation we might imagine. Each name is a new variation on an old signifier, and each signifier needs deconstruction, but because we are fickle humans it's simply easier to submit without a second thought. And truth be told, even rethinking itself can be a placeholder keeping the Master Signifier hidden from view. Whether or not we purchase fair trade coffee may let us change ourselves from uncaring consumer to ethically conscious consumer, but we are still consumers all the same. We are desiring machines. We eat, we breathe, and we heat.

Even the most confident ideas will change with time. If anything is malleable, it may be reshaped. We don't think of the tallest building as malleable, but from time to time metal heats into liquid and foundations crack. Like the nations and religions constructing them, every structure will fall to the ground in time.

The apostle's wordplay—neither this category nor that—aims at something: all our assumed signifiers are a bit of a farce. We already know it, we fight against it, and don't want to hear it. As Derrida's philosophy taught us, there is no law that reaches the ideal of Justice. Indeed, there may be some real Master Signifier called sin or progress or capitalism working behind it all. If we desire to stretch out toward some ideal of Justice or Truth, we had best think on how our justices and truths actually act as a barrier. Let us meditate on our sins.

I'm not simply saying that those who claim they know the Truth are fooling themselves. My claim goes further: the braggarts and arrogant guardians of the supposed Truth *know* they are lying to themselves. They are the tribe of certainty. Their protests are as strong as their doubts, and their outward confidence screams as loud as their inward anxiety. They know, and they don't want you to know that they know. Have nothing to do with them.

The End

In a moment, there was nothing but utter darkness. In a split second that seems an eternity, you begin to comprehend your life has ended, and you have passed on. The dark hue brightens until you find yourself in a room of pure light, with only yourself and an elderly figure sitting across from you. Waves of emotion keep you from speaking for days, as you had never quite faced the reality that you would eventually die. But finally you gather the your wits to ask where you are. The old man shifts uneasily, considering how to answer such a meaningless question until at last he answers, "Friend, you are where you have always been."

A lifetime of questions come flooding back to you, wondering about paradise and punishment. You wonder aloud, "Am I here to wait for something?"

Disappointedly, the elder elaborates, "My friend, your existence is not a place, and neither are you coming or going, nor being made to wait for anything."

An eternity passes, but to every question, you are greeted with only a similarly cryptic response. Your striving eats away at your soul. As eternity passes on, you realize your striving is meaningless, which is where your wonderings have always been. You come to peace with this eventually.

After a good while, the elder, no longer interrupted by your questions, stands with a smile and says to you, "It is finished. I can see you are finished." He leads you to two doors and, gesturing to the first, says you may enter through it to return to an eternal, dreamless, serene sleep.

The alternate door lies adjacent, with the words inscribed above: *Abandon hope all ye who enter.*

"And what of the streets of gold and the heavenly mansions our elders spoke of?" you ask. Feelings of indignation rise as you angrily fight the suspicion your end has indeed arrived.

"Yes, I have walked those streets," the figure replies. "There are those that need an eternity chasing luxuries before they can rest. But if you desire your striving, that is the second door."

5 Illusion and Delusion, Prophecy and Apocalypse

We are rediscovering today what the prophets told us long ago: what we cannot bear to feel during the day will haunt our dreams by night. What cannot be remembered will be repeated in our behavior. What cannot be spoken aloud will be ingrained in our rituals. We are as creative as we are fearful. Our creativity is a field from which we reap sustenance, but it is also the factory packaging denial of all we fear to be true.

This chapter begins with prophets and ends in apocalypse. As I've said from the start, I am interested in the flood beginning when we question our most basic assumptions. I am more interested in how ideas work than where they arrive. I am interested in how a question about ancient Israel— those who called themselves wanderers in the desert—turns so quickly into a question about modern immigration policy. I am interested in how a question about Christ's atonement challenges the nature of forgiveness, and I am interested in how the erasure of guilt changes our thinking about our student loan debts. I am interested in how Saint Augustine's abstract doctrine of original sin informs our nation's concrete original sin of slavery, or how a story of violence in a book written twenty-five hundred years ago becomes justification for a war today. I am interested in how rethinking our closest religious beliefs changes our thinking about everything else. And I am also interested in why so many dare not think.

The truth has the structure of a fiction, but I have no interest in simply pulling a rug of certainty out from under our fleeting feet. My goal is much worse, for every view we hold is everywhere and always a misdirection, a placeholder, a false consciousness seeking to avoid. We believe things because reality construction is human. We choose not to reconsider our beliefs if we desire to blend into our tribes. Those with eyes to see and ears to hear and hearts to ache for the oppressed will not fit the tribe of certainty. The tribe would rather change things just enough so that everything can stay the same.

So it went that Ezekiel found himself bound like a fool on his side, staring at the model of Jerusalem before it was sacked and cooking his food atop a burning pile of his own excrement. His rage burned against the sins of Sodom, which he told us was an overfed culture of arrogance with no concern for the poor.[1] We prefer to think the sins of Sodom were something else, because if the sins of Sodom were, in fact, being overfed and unconcerned, we would have to face our own recklessness. So it was that Isaiah walked the halls of power to whisper of its approaching collapse. He bit the hand that fed him, and he spoke to people whose ears and eyes were closed and blinded. He spoke to a nation on the verge of implosion, and the prideful cannot afford to listen to warnings. So it went as well when the Christ began his teaching in a quiet synagogue with an unwelcome message: who really desires redistribution for the poor, sight for the blind, and freedom from oppression when present conditions are the very foundation of the *status quo*?

As we've seen, the dogmatic religious types never seem to notice what their supposed savior thought of dogmatic religious types. It's far easier to concoct a version of the Christ who loved certainty, so long as it is the correct certainty (always filled with godlike arrogance and unconcern). And just as the message of the prophets was lost on ancient ears—for things do not change so much from epoch to epoch—we close our eyes and ears because we'd rather not know about ourselves. The message we evade sinks deep into our unconscious and keeps the social machine running. The message becomes grafted into our rituals and behavior, into our issues and causes, into our anger and hope. What cannot be accepted and remembered will return in an inverted form.

We gather together to break bread and drink wine, but we forget the original act of the Eucharist was an invitation for communion, a feast without regard for social class, and fundamentally an act redistributing the grace that naturally goes along with sharing a meal. We took a holy act and turned it into a litmus test for an in-group, and in so doing we re-crucify the body broken for us. The conversion of Eucharist from gift to litmus test

---

1. See Ezek 16:49.

48

happened quickly, for it is no mystery that an in-group quickly jumps to police its boundaries. What cannot be properly remembered (grace, redistribution, and emancipation) becomes repressed in a vain ritual, a ritual organized around anxiety in an inverted form of the ritual's original meaning.

Diogenes the Cynic was once asked why people give alms to the poor but not to philosophers. He guessed they give to the poor and the blind because they think they may become poor and blind, but nobody expects to suddenly start thinking. Indeed, if you have ever gone down the path of rethinking something fundamental to your tribe, you understand what I mean when I claim daring to think is one of the most antisocial acts imaginable. We become the rubbish that must be repressed so our tribe may continue to sleep. The saints know this well, for as we have seen, a saint is always an empty signifier. Saints cannot be remembered without offense, so they are converted into misrecognized dreams and misremembered parodies.

Misremembering Origins

When I teach my students the history of Christian and Jewish thought, we look at the dual creation stories of Genesis chapters one and two, and we compare them with the ancient Babylonian story called *Enuma Elish* ("When On High"). In the Babylonian myth, the parents of the gods become angry at their children for being too loud and decide to slay them. Enraged at this plot, the wise god Ea and the warrior god Marduk battle against their parent gods, and after the war is over Marduk creates the heavens and the earth (in roughly the same order copied in Genesis chapter one). He pours out the blood of an enemy god and creates humankind out of the divine blood. We know this version is from a tablet in Babylon, because Babylon worshiped Marduk. In ancient Mesopotamia, each city's version of the creation myth presents its own god as the protagonist. It is a story Judah encountered during its exile in Babylon, a period in the sixth century BCE when Jewish scribes were organizing the Hebrew Bible, and they made the story their own. But in the Jewish version, God was deeply good and fashioned humankind from the dust of the earth rather than the blood of a demon. And then my class asks: do we still have creation myths today?

I teach the viral spread of myths with this example. In ten thousand years, an archaeologist from New Earth descends in a rocket to land in the old deserts of Iraq. She finds a document containing a story about a great and generous leader, who desired peace so much he gave up all his weapons, who was so honest he had to tell his father when he chopped down a cherry tree, who tried in vain to defend his people against a foreign emperor, and whose name was Hussein. The archaeologist knows of a war between the West and the Middle East in this period, so it would be no great leap to assume who Hussein and the foreign emperor were. And from where would the story of the chopped cherry tree come?

Ancient myths almost always transfer from a more powerful culture to a less powerful culture, and when they transfer they are modified to the liking of the adopting city. In a previous version of the *Enuma Elish*, perhaps the older Sumerian god Ea was the protagonist. But even though Sumerians invented writing in 3200 BCE, the version we have is Babylonian, and it *misremembers* the story. Just as we saw in my story of Washington's features being misremembered, the story a culture tells itself about its great leaders is always a misremembering. America's creation myth involves intellectuals who were also brutal slaveholders. This is not new information; it is something we have agreed to forget. Creation myths are all around us, from our religions to our nations to the stories we trade about our friends and family. Every tribe has its creation myths, and they are always illusions guarding against knowing too much.

Lest we drive into the ravine of skepticism, let us hit the brakes to consider what we do know. Yes, all truth has the structure of a fiction, for we believe with immense certainty so many things that are not true, but what help is it to recognize this? All this philosophizing is still a waste of time if we cannot come out of this with a few things we do know. Let us propose we think of our beliefs in three broad ways: (1) wish versus indifference, (2) anxiety versus security, and (3) factual versus delusional.

First, we must recognize a spectrum of from our *wishes* to our *indifference*.[2] We have very little difficulty letting go of doctrines—no matter how crucial they once appeared to be—if we haven't any wish for them to be true. We tenaciously and aggressively hold on to the thing we desire.

Second, we need to acknowledge a spectrum of destabilized *anxiety* to absolute *security*. Religion is filled with desire, and it is simply better suited to providing security than to inciting the quest for truth.[3] We feel the anxiety of not knowing, and we search for the one who will say he (and

---

2. I use the words *wish* and *desire* interchangeably throughout this book.

3. I should credit my professor Lori Anne Ferrell for teaching me "religion is desire." It was such a simple observation with such profound consequences.

is it not usually a he rather than a she?) knows the absolute Truth. But rather than saying we simply seek certainty, I want to argue we actually *do* desire the anxiety and ambiguity justifying a lack of determined choice. For example, when I drive away from home but obsess over whether or not I turned off the oven's gas, it is almost as if I trick myself into believing my house could not explode until I make up my mind whether or not to return. We like to think the universe will forgive us while we are still in the process of deciding, thus the small comfort we feel in a moment of anxiety, of ambiguity, and even of mystery tells us what we'd prefer not to know. Not knowing is an inverted form of knowing. For example, when someone tells you "I believe X, but I don't want to think it all the way through—I'd rather keep my simple faith," she is admitting her security in *not* knowing. In other words, *not* knowing is itself a type of certainty, but it is toxic and won't ultimately work.

Third, only then may we arrive at the typical question of whether a religious belief is *factual* or *delusional*. The great many who dismiss religion altogether as outdated mythmaking normally start here, but their arguments fall on deaf ears precisely because they have not accounted for the reasons we still believe in the face of all evidence to the contrary. We can ask why we believe foolish things all day long while ignoring deeper questions of why.

Spectrums: Our Wishes and Our Indifference

To consider how beliefs are shaped by wishes or desires, let's use an example from our history books. When Columbus set sail across the oceans, it was a gamble. Nobody knew whether it would pay off, least of all the men aboard the boats. Learned men and women had in fact known for thousands of years that the earth was round, but this knowledge hadn't reached the sailors as they embarked on their journey. It is not unheard of for a great wealth of knowledge to go missing. After all, knowledge is a powerful technology, and sometimes it is withheld by those in power. When those in power realized the earth was round, it meant global resources were finite. I do not mean to suggest a grand plot, but is there not a certain pattern to the suppression of knowledge for the sake of profit? We learned the world no longer stretched unchanging in all directions, and—if the round-earthers were to be believed—colonizing far enough in one direction would lead right back to the empire's doorstep. Accumulation became a zero-sum game. The same class would later insist climate science was a hoax, because a public awakened to truth would injure their profit margins. In their cruel selfishness they slashed corporate taxes while binding the funding of public education to local property taxes, ensuring children born in poorer neighborhoods wouldn't have a fighting chance. They haven't any use for equality. They would convince those they saw as plebeians that the teachers and professors were overpaid elitists whose work should be scorned. They haven't any use for critical thinking. The pattern is as haphazard as it is lucrative: when knowledge is missing—when we lack the ability to articulate how unfree we are, when we view our unfreedom as deserved—the voracious hunger for wealth roams free and preys upon the earth's limited resources. Consequently, Europe set out to colonize the world and claim every last resource for its own ends. Columbus did not wish to find a New World. He merely wished to find a shorter route to the Indies. It must be difficult to desire something so badly that the discovery of a New World instead was actually a nuisance.

It's not entirely clear what Columbus believed he found (or re-found, as it's clearly wrong to say Europe discovered what others had long inhabited). There is some evidence to suggest Columbus was aware he had stumbled upon new lands, and there is the possibility he ignored this for ulterior motives, or perhaps he simply refused to accept the novelty. At any rate, he spoke of finding not what he had actually found but instead what he wished to have found. This suggests something peculiar about wish fulfillment, for interrupting history by discovering a New World was nothing compared to his wish to succeed on a path he began. Few others at the time had Columbus's difficulty, and a great many realized we had found something new. The difference between Columbus and everyone else from the epoch was simply in the wish (or lack thereof), because seeing with wishful desire is not the same as seeing without desire.

The psychoanalyst Freud taught the terms *illusion* and *delusion* for what we see in Columbus.[4] An illusion is a belief propped up with a wish. Whether the belief is right or wrong is irrelevant for the moment, because the illusion gives us security. Illusions are what we wish to see. It is like a mirage in the desert—we see water when our thirst must be quenched. No thirsty desert traveler sees a mirage of fire.

---

4. For further reading on illusion and delusion, as well as the examples I give, see Freud, *The Future of an Illusion*.

What Columbus also teaches us is that evidence itself is no weapon against the shield of a wish or desire. Why do some people change their religious, moral, or political minds with ease while others do not? Is it just a matter of intellect? Certainly not. While we occasionally change our minds with new evidence, psychological research (not to mention our everyday experience) suggests that contradictory evidence merely entrenches old ideas further into their battle lines. The cause that gets up and leaves the battle is the idea for which we no longer wished to fight. People lose beliefs not when they are disproved but when they no longer wish them to be true.

Modern neuropsychology has made a fascinating discovering about our reactions to ideas contrary to our own. If we were to put ourselves into an fMRI machine and then listen to ideas with which we disagree, we would see increased activity in the amygdala and other parts of the brain controlling the fight-or-flight mechanism. In short, when we hear a dis-agreeable idea, the body's chemical reaction is the same as if someone had pulled a knife on us in a dark alley. We don't consciously feel so threatened over disagreements, but nevertheless the body begins to pump adrenaline into the muscles, and—much more importantly—the prefrontal cortex (which controls rational cognition) goes darker. Though some exhibit this reaction stronger than others, this basic reaction to disagreeable ideas is universal to humans. Another way to put it is this: if we claim strange ideas never make us angry, we are either lying to ourselves or revealing we have a malfunctioning brain. We can safely bet on the former; we simply don't like to think of ourselves as reactionary, emotional beings who can't think rationally.

This is the way illusion works, the belief sustained by a desiring wish. But on the other hand we should explore the delusion, the objectively false belief. When we say someone has "delusions of grandeur" it is because they think themselves great when they are not. When someone claims they have seen a ghost, we call this delusional only if we already assume there are (as a matter of accepted fact) no such things as ghosts. It is important to think through the difference, for a single belief can be (1) illusion or (2) delusion, and it can be (3) both or (4) neither. There are also going to be cases where we cannot yet say, but perhaps we will be able to say in the future. Let us consider a few more examples.

The case of Columbus teaches us what it looks like for a belief to be both illusion and delusion. His belief that he had found a new route to the East was illusion, because he clearly wished to succeed in finding the route.

But the belief was a delusion inasmuch as he simply didn't find what he sought. The objective fact was that he encountered something else, islands on the edge of a New World. The existence of wish and falsehood in equal measure make Columbus a case of illusion and delusion.

On the far other side of the equation are beliefs that are neither illusions nor delusions, such as when I believe the earth revolves around the sun. I have no particular wish for this to be the case, but so it is. We needn't carelessly careen so far down the rabbit hole of humility to make every judgement relative. There are facts out there in the world, but very few of our important decisions and beliefs are based on facts alone.

Consider the joke telling of an Englishman who was so brave he not only had no fear of ghosts, he didn't even believe in them. In matters of illusion and delusion, there is wide and peculiar space between both and neither, in the very space mixing wishes and lack of wishes, facts and falsehoods. This joke suggests we might say we don't believe X and yet act as if we do. We might say we don't believe in ghosts or hell and yet fear them. We might say we don't believe in fate and yet fear we will end up just like our parents. In between the illusion and delusion is where things become interesting, and it is where all theology argues itself into the ground. The question is whether an idea is true but also whether we wish it to be true, for the wish will cloud our judgment.

A great debate has stirred over whether same-sex marriage should be allowed or prohibited. Even now as our courts in the United States have issued their decree, is it not interesting to consider how Christianity will adjust? Will it hold its ground on the decree of biblicism or change as it has in the past? It is a question for the sociologists and the political scientists, who likely already know the answer. Our interest is rather with how and why people's opinions change.

Many well-meaning and foolish people say they believe in absolute Truth and detest so-called relativism. But their unwillingness to think about how their own values are relativized—indexed to their time, location, class, and anything else attributable to their birth—shows those who profess absolutism are often (if unconsciously) the most relativist at all. The philosopher and theologian Alfred North Whitehead once remarked how interesting it is when the so-called guardians of morality are the most likely to flee away from the new. One would think those who desire a more moral society would be ever-striving for the highest-reaching ideals, but instead of seeing a new moment as a time to expand and grow, the momentous occasion is turned into a time of retreat. The retreat into older ideas has an important consistency to it—after all, if we had things right before, we shouldn't tamper with it now. But this perspective errs when it closes its ears to those protesting, those who say their experience of a religio-cultural tradition was harmful. So the traditionalist, while aiming to preserve a noble goal, will not hear the protests of those hurt by a noble goal. Illusion is at work here, for it is not the highest ideal we seek to preserve but instead the wish for the world to never change. The so-called guardians of morality are those who are fundamentally opposed to the idea that anything new could happen.

Some religious beliefs can be verified as true or false, for whether or not the earth was created in seven days is a claim to be put to the scientific test. Such claims can be put into the bins of delusion or truth. Moral judgements are seldom like this. We are not speaking of something suitable for the scientific test, so the question of delusion is not in play. In contrast, it is rather obvious that, in a debate about civil rights, the contest between our so-called traditional family values and our desire for equality is a contest of wishes, not facts. So while we firmly believe our position is just, we can't deny it is also an illusion held aloft by a wish.

The theologian Paul Tillich noticed we aren't simply divided into relativist and absolutists when it comes to values. Instead, we are always a mix of both, and it is often those most opposed to relativism who have drifted furthest into relativism (those who wish so badly to be correct that they ignore anything to the contrary). But Tillich also noticed there are both positive and negative versions of both (1) relativism and (2) absolutism. The (1a) positive version of relativism embraces new perspectives and values, but a (1b) negative relativism rejects all values. The (2a) positive version of absolutism is revolutionary, but a (2b) negative absolutism is authoritarian and uncaring. So we can say we are both relativist and absolutist, provided we hold on to the idealism claiming our world could be better. We would still be filled with illusions, but we would be open to rethinking at all times. We would have our work cut out for us, for the guardians of morality are there to criticize our relativism when they are absolutist and our absolutism when they are relativist. In any case, a perspective that resists falling for its own illusions would be one that is always open to the new, always on the edge of the flood of questions upsetting our illusions and delusions.

In my experience, maintaining or discarding beliefs has very little to do with the question of factuality and delusion. When we consider whether or not to abandon a previously crucial belief, it's rarely a question of facts. It's more a question of whether or not we like the version of ourselves we see emerging—the version that no longer wishes to believe something. We maintain the most repressive and deeply self-destructive values, because we have an unconscious wish for the belief to remain in place. But for those wishing to change their beliefs, the problem is different. Those who wish for the new often need nothing more than the ratification of some source of authority—a person, a community, or a sacred book on occasion. We desire a big Other to tell us we are fine. Even though our entire identities may be tied into believing a certain thing, to leave behind our repressive ideas once their allure has faded *should* be a most simple and natural act.

Spectrums: Our Anxiety and Our Security

If we can successfully parse out our illusions and delusions, then the next item to which we must turn our attention is the spectrum from anxiety to security. Recall the example of how we feel when, after leaving our houses in the morning, we suspect (but aren't yet sure) we might have left a gas oven on. We feel an odd type of assuredness or security while we are deciding whether we really need to return home. We might imagine our houses couldn't explode for the moment, and it is only *after* we have decided we should return home to check the gas that we feel certain danger. Clearly, we are in the most dangerous position while we are doing nothing and continuing to debate in our heads whether or not we should return home. But instead of feeling danger while we debate, many people actually feel the opposite. We feel safest in ambiguity, not certainty. We prefer the awkward certainty found in the very ground of ambiguity, and gods are not so different from gas ovens.

Anxiety is not doubt; it is the *cause* of doubt.[5] They say anxiety is fear without object, but that's not quite right. In a sense, it would be more accurate to say anxiety always exists in relation to a specifically feared object, but the object is often imaginary. Consider how we feel anxious over everyone's judgement even when nobody is actually judging us. We feel anxious over our obsessive questions and the answers that never arrive. It matters very little whether question is eternal or mundane, whether God exists or if

5. My understanding of the nature of anxiety is thoroughly indebted to Jacques Lacan's tenth seminar. His claim "anxiety is the cause of doubt" is found in Lacan, *Anxiety*, 76.

the bank account will dry up before the end of the month—anxiety inflicts its wrath upon our sleep cycle regardless. The object of our anxiety can be irrelevant, arbitrary, imaginary, and even pointless. Our hearts race without an appropriate scale, for when we are anxious we are simply anxious. We did not evolve to become appropriately anxious at the proper time for precise reasons in reasonable measure. We evolved to fear even without object.

In an ancient wilderness, two of our ancestors heard a rustling in the bushes. One feared an evil spirit and ran, while the other fearlessly stood his ground. The first felt foolish, for the rustling was only the wind. On the next day, the two ancestors again heard a rustling in the bushes, and again the fearful man fled. But on this day, the gene for courage was swallowed up into the belly of a saber-toothed tiger. In the ancestor who survived, anxiety without object cemented itself into the genes passed down to us today. It's been called a *hypersensitive agency detection device*,[6] which means our ancestors were simply better off expecting wild animals and evil spirits acting everywhere, even when there was nothing to fear but the wind. Only the fearful get out alive.

Over the ages, the same violence weeding out a brave gene also stamped out our impulse to see humanity in our the neighbors. It's much easier to barricade ourselves inside the walls of the known, to leave ambiguous mysteries undefiled, and to call our ambiguity humility. Rituals helped us deal with the anxiety, for religion has always had two—and ultimately only two—uses: (1) the personal explanation where there can be none and (2) keeping the tribe together. If I critique your faith and you feel anxiety, it's because I struck against one of those purposes.

In the beginning, there was only anxiety. It spread because it was a caring mother, and it's now worshiped in the very rituals that were supposed to suppress it. We never really suppress anything. Instead we repress, we keep it out of sight, but the repressed will always return with brute force. The walls we erected to protect us from anxiety were called rituals, and rituals became religions. Religions became doctrines, and doctrines became exclusion. Exclusion became certainty, and certainty became further anxiety.

I have yet to meet a person whose faithful certainty is not doubt-ridden, but I have met people a great number of people who seem completely unaware of their doubts. They display their anxiety with every fiber

---

6. Many have written at length about the evolution of the hypersensitive agency detection device. For further reading on how it affects moral values, I recommend chapter 11 of Haidt, *The Righteous Mind*.

of their being—the way they carry themselves, the usual arguments they've pocketed, the flash of anger that cannot be tamed however much they try. I cannot fault them for it, for it is how I was once trained to think as well.

Certainty always excludes, but it is also a peculiar kind of safety. It never feels secure, but it seems to be as close as we are going to get to security. My assumption when meeting the fundamentalist is not that I must convince he or she is wrong—my assumption is she already knows. She already feels the flaws, which is why she searches the Internet and the prayer circles for excuses to continue unchanged. We didn't evolve to have rational conversations, for this is only a recent phenomenon. We evolved to attack whatever is different. And while it may seem anxiety is a place of great unknowing, in another manner of speaking it's the *only* place where we have no doubt whatsoever. Anxiety is the only emotional affect that never lies. Anxiety is not doubt. Anxiety is the cause of doubt.

This is because anxiety is an ambivalent middle ground between where we are and what we imagine we desire. The advantage of ambivalence is that we needn't make a choice. This is why the fundamentalist resists any knowledge contradicting what she wishes to believe. She thinks she desires certainty and detests ambiguity, but in fact her security is tied to ambiguity, to the refusal to ask why she feels such anxiety about her fundamentalism. When we are told what to believe or do or love, we have the choice made for us. When we begin to suspect the imposed idea is a farce, we have a choice to make. For many, the ambivalent middle ground is a fine new home, for it keeps us safe from the looming confrontation with our doubts. But doubt is there, staring at us from the other side of the chasm. We didn't ask for doubt; it simply happens or it doesn't. We might choose whether to foster or repress doubts through the books we read and the conversations we entertain, but it is not up to us. People do not choose their beliefs. Their beliefs happen to them, and when they happen those beliefs can be repressed or embraced.

We don't walk ourself to the edge of doubt, for this is already done for us. Our choice is rather to either (1) remain in our place by repressing what we suspect true or (2) cast aside ideas that do not work. It is the middle space between the two—of anxiety and her sister called ambivalence—where things become intriguing. The theologically invested word for ambivalence is *mystery*, and labeling an irredeemably problematic idea as a mystery (and simply leaving it there) is a way to resist rethinking. Isn't it odd how whatever gets itself called mystery always seems to be quite certain? We want to call it a mystery because we desire to appear both orthodox and reflective, and in the meantime we've simply resisted thought and called it humility.

Take the example of the Christian doctrine of the Trinity. At the Council of Nicaea in 325 CE, bishops from across the Roman Empire gathered together at the behest of Emperor Constantine to decide for the first time on a standardized creed in which all Christians must believe. Constantine had recently defeated three other regional Roman rulers and secured his sole rule over the empire, but after his conversion to Christianity in 312 CE and his Edict of Milan a year later, which granted toleration of the Christian faith throughout the empire, he had a new problem: infighting among the various bishops might well tear the empire apart. It was the beginning of Christendom (the merger of Christianity and kingdom), and if the church and state were going to be married there would need to be an agreement on what the relationship meant.

The bishop Arius and his followers were teaching "there was a time when the Christ was not." In other words, if Christ was the only begotten son of God, then there must have been a time when Christ did not yet exist. The bishop Athanasius countered Arius and assumed Christ had always existed. Emperor Constantine probably cared very little who won the debate, but if he wanted to rule a united empire, he needed to calm the theological storm. So he convened the first ecumenical council at Nicaea to settle the debate, and the result was a creed with a new Trinity—a term never found in the Bible but which was now the starting point for Christian orthodoxy.

I'm less interested in the particulars of orthodoxy and heresy and more interested in the motivation dividing orthodoxies and heresies. Later, at the Council of Constantinople in 380 CE, the three highly influential Cappadocian Fathers—Gregory of Nyssa, Gregory of Nazianzus, and Basil the Great—developed the idea of Trinity further. The question on everyone's mind was whether the three parts of the Trinity (Father, Son, and Holy Spirit) were three gods, three persons, three modes that God could variously take, or merely three office duties. When someone likens the persons of the Trinity to an egg's shell, white, and yolk, or when the Trinity is likened to water's liquid, ice, and steam states, they are thinking in terms of modes. This was precisely what the Cappadocian Fathers would investigate and later call heresy.

Instead they claimed the three persons of Father, Son, and Holy Spirit are one substance, God, in three persons. Each is fully God, and God is fully each. In normal language, we understand one person cannot stand in the same place as any other(s), but they decided the Trinity was an exception to this rule; essentially, the Trinity was the only space in the universe where three persons could occupy the same position. It wasn't of much interest whether this was possible, and neither did they feel much need to explain it. It was simply called a mystery, and confessing this mystery became the starting point for all Christian orthodoxy thereafter. Interestingly enough, the Cappadocian Fathers who wrote the Trinity—this standard of orthodoxy—where also apparently universalists who believed all go to paradise. When universalism itself was later proclaimed a heresy, we arrive at an interesting turning point for Christianity: the writers of the purest orthodoxy were also retroactively decided to be deceived heretics.

None of this means mystery itself is an error, but we should recognize mystery cannot exist without ambiguity or ambivalence. Mystery is what we call whatever we'd rather avoid reconsidering. We avoid because avoidance delivers a false security and fights off anxiety. Ambiguity shields us from making a decision, and ambivalence protects us from caring about the decision. The mystery may be true; but if it is false, would we know or even care? Mystery is the synonym of ambivalence. Ambivalence is the sister of anxiety. Ambivalence is not indifferent or unconcerned. When someone expresses ambivalence at a question, it's often because examining the question would be unbearable. When the psychoanalyst asks a patient about her father and she parries the question with ambivalence, we can be sure the question hit the nail on the head. It is rather when she is indifferent to the question (when she can discuss her father without deflecting) that anxiety has truly ceased. Religion is like this too, for there is a wide difference between questions that must be avoided and the authentic answer that can be embraced.

And so the neurotic returns home to make sure the gas oven is off. She is anxious, which is borne out in her repetitive drive home. She would like you to think she is reasonable, calculating the best course of action on this day, but overall she wants you to think she was indifferent and not too concerned. But it was her anxiety driving her doubts, and, in a sense, knowing we are anxious is the only thing we ever certainly know at all. Anxiety is a signal: something is not working.

Spectrums: Our Facts and Our Delusions

There is a child's game where the parent sings "The dog goes woof-woof, the cat goes meow-meow"[7] and continues on with however many animals the parent desires to impersonate. As the mother sings the song faster and faster, she inevitably slips—"The dog goes meow-meow"—and the child takes great delight in catching and correcting the slip. From our earliest moments, something in us desires repetition. Repetition is normally harmless in infants but a cause for psychotherapy later when it leads to repeatedly bad jobs, relationships, and habits. What would it mean to think of our theology as exactly this kind of repetition?

One of my favorite quotes from Freud is, "The voice of intellect is a soft one, but it does not rest until it gains a hearing."[8] But most people don't have much use for expertise, and they'd rather persist with delusions rather than fact the facts. We desire things to change just enough so things can remain basically the same. We see all around us, everyday, the effects of opinion without content. Content-free opinion infects everything from our social media news feeds to our global policy makers. Those without the hunger for knowledge feel free to yell over the timid voice of reason. Is it even worth asking whether content-free opinion infects our theology as well?

Opinion is a weapon of mass destruction, and no precision weapon of knowledge will surmount it. Opinion is filled with desire, and it's shielded with confirmation bias and armed with misappropriated statistics. While the confirmation bias is often destructive, it is also deeply necessary, for if we don't commit to any perspective, then we are swayed too easily. We haven't a choice in whether we either do or don't have an ideology—we have only the choice of accepting the normative ideology or questioning it. This is what I tell those who say there isn't much use in philosophy. To refuse critical thinking is simply to submit to someone else's cunning. As the saying goes, there are lies, damned lies, and statistics. Even the facts of the matter, when manipulated into the right context, will mislead every gazing eye. Every illusionist knows this, and the job of the magician involves taking the desire of the audience to be fooled and producing a trick we will enjoy. Think on this, for we actually enjoy believing even when we

---

7. This example is from Lacan, *Écrits*, 593 and 682.
8. Freud, *The Future of an Illusion*, 93.

know—without a shadow of doubt and without a moment's confusion—what we witness and believe cannot be.

We previously discussed Freud's grandson as he played a game whose sole purpose was distracting himself from what he knew to be true. The mother was missing. The thing he needed was not where it should be, but the infant enjoyed it all the same. Let's consider another childhood example similar to the dog-cat song. Let's take a parent who reads a story aloud to a child one night, and every night afterward the child demands the same story be read again. The parent relents and lovingly retells the story from the book, but in order to keep things interesting, the parent begins to add new parts to the story. The mother enjoys her creative storytelling, and the child enjoys noticing the changes, catching the parent and forcing her to admit what she just said wasn't really in the book. The game between the parent and child continues this way until the child tires of the book and graduates to a new story, where they will continue to play this game until the child can read.

What is the meaning of this example? We might notice this same "gotcha!" campaign played in childhood never really ends. Isn't much of our adulthood invested in noticing the hypocritical slips of the politician, the priest, and the CEO? Yes, indeed it's an easy connection to make, but anyone who has played this reading game with a child will know the game did not stop simply at catching changes.

Instead, the child begins to prefer certain novel additions to the story. Or put differently, we *prefer* the delusion. The child may consciously know the new addition is not held in the pages of the book and yet prefer to hear the new version every time the story is retold. The adult never knows what story the child will prefer, for childish desires are king and queen when deciding how history is written. We may know the story is a fiction, merely a farce contrived for someone's entertainment (or agenda), but does knowledge really matter if we actually prefer the altered version of reality? Likewise for political and theological ideologues, things must change just enough so they remain basically the same.

What does this look like in the political realm? Let's quickly revisit our earlier discussion of symptom and cause. To change things just enough so they can remain the same is the mode of addressing symptoms instead of root causes. Some illnesses cannot be adequately defeated by treating a root cause, and this is often perfectly fine. For example, while the common cold is incurable in terms of killing the virus itself, our bodies are able to fight off the virus while our medicines simply treat symptoms. Occasionally addressing symptoms is all that's necessary. However, nobody prescribes aspirin to treat a headache brought on by a brain tumor. Sometimes addressing the symptom alone is deadly.

Politics is very often exactly this confusion of symptom and cause, and a campaign attacking symptoms (which are so very easy to see) is a much more winning strategy. Treating the cause would require deep reflection on complex cause-effect networks, but this wouldn't fit into a sound bite. So we dismiss thoughtful reflection as the expert's snobby elitism when we'd rather not think about actual causes. This is easier than ever in the era of mass information. When the Internet began to spread in the 1990s, journalists speculated that massive access to information would revolutionize democracy. What happened instead was information glut. Overwhelmed with the sheer amount of data, we sequestered ourselves to only reading the sources we already trusted. The result was that the Left and the Right, the vegan and the omnivore, the Christian and the atheist, the egalitarian and the fascist—all of them read a different set of news, and all of their confirmation biases arose with a vengeance.

In fact, though this is not widely recognized, it now appears Google—which tailors search results with an algorithm sensitive to a number of factors tied to a user—actually returns slightly different answers to questions typed by liberals and conservatives. Even the location of the user affects results. Though location-sensitive results are harmless when searching for a particular restaurant, the results might be drastic if location is used as a proxy for education, race, or income. Researchers have called this a geolocal Filter Bubble Effect.[9] It is not merely a case of television viewers preferring Fox or CNN or MSNBC. Even the same question typed into a smartphone will return truths relative to our biases. We pray our searches to Google, and it gives us what we seek. As a result, an unmerited conspiracy theory can become the absolute Truth for a whole segment of society. Politicians must then play along, pretending they will do something about a problem that literally doesn't exist while actual problems continue unabated. Why treat the cancer with anything more than aspirin when the vast cancers of society won't kill us for at least another generation?

So everyone considers themselves an expert, and those with actual expertise can become seen as arrogant elitists. This process opens up space for content-free opinion, content-free opinion opens rages against symptoms

9. See Klinman-Silver et al., "Location, Location, Location."

instead of causes, and eventually the cancer marches forth across the body. The cancer finds a friend in leaders who cynically lie about symptoms. It finds support in those who foolishly doubt the science of cancers. Are we stressed over these symptoms?—we are told to have a drink or a smoke to take the edge off the stress and carry on with our lives.

Again, it's ironic how those who protest loudest against relativism are so often opposed to philosophers who study truth. On the one hand we haven't much need to discuss a difference of fact and farce, for it is all too clear there are things so painfully and obviously false. But on the other hand we might suggest our supposedly enlightened, postmodern age is ill-equipped to call out the farce of the cynic for what it is. We are told it's too brash, too impolite, or too arrogant to talk about the motives of someone else (even when it's plain what their motives are). In a manner of speaking, I agree wholeheartedly: I don't care about the conscious justifications or personal traumas causing a leader to lie or a follower to be fooled. But I do care about the actual effects of those cynical lies upon the world we inhabit. We rightly attacked the arrogance of absolute Truth, but we seemed to think a post-absolute path should coexist with the fact-free lies. If someone causes harm, we shouldn't fear calling him a liar.

In the same way that every war has two sides—the defense and the preemptive defense (does anyone ever consider themselves the attacker?)—there is always a justification for the deception, for the lie, and for the delusional farce. Maybe an infant desires her parents to read a book, but she wants them to change it as well. Maybe we desire honesty from our beloved, but sometimes we only want support. Maybe we feel no conscious prejudice whatsoever, and yet our racism permeates our society. Maybe we desire equality for everyone, and yet our patriarchy suppresses half the population. Maybe we love the sinner and hate the sin, and yet our action is no different than if we hated all along.

I don't say we should dismiss a person's motives, which are always crafted to protect our fragile egos from horror. I'm arguing we can speak of unconscious reality, we can speak the truth in love (precisely because of love), and that this is an entirely different matter from how we consciously justify the unjustifiable. We must discern truth and falsehoods, and we must name our lies when they issue forth from our mouths. To do this, we must bear in mind that truth and falsehood is skin deep. Underneath the surface lies—in both meanings of the term—all our wishes and anxieties, and occasionally nothing more than misinformation. To have eyes to see, as the Hebrew prophets always advised, means we should have eyes piercing through the imaginary dimensions that veil what hides beneath.

We Desire Our Demise: This Is the Way the World Ends

The philosopher Slavoj Žižek rightly says it's easier to imagine the end of the world than to imagine modest changes to capitalism. The Hollywood filmmaker can envision any number of ways for the world to end—from natural phenomena of supermassive comets and earthquakes to the fantastic zombie apocalypses and alien invasions—but cannot imagine a world in which basic necessities were guaranteed.[10] Why? It isn't simply that we lack imagination, for we aren't too short on proposals to resolve our economic antagonisms. The horrific truth is precisely the opposite: we are attracted to the idea of destruction. We have a death drive. Our climate is collapsing without our concern while our cinemas and preachers dream up imaginary threats to capture our attention.

If our most closely held beliefs are illusions, held aloft by an unconscious wish for them to be true, what does this suggest about theology? It would be simple, easy, and wrong to conclude theology is nothing more than wish fulfillment, for we do seem to believe a great many things we detest. For example, a person may say "I do not like the idea that my friends and relatives who do not believe as I do will spend eternity in a torturous hell." Some believe this because they are told they must believe this, and they experience enormous angst at the prospect. But there are also those who are not consciously lying when they say this, and yet everything about their existence suggests the *do* wish the worst for those who are different. If the interpretation of theology as illusion or delusion (or both or neither) hinges on our unconscious wishes, what can any of this tell us concretely about the nature of our beliefs? Let us take an example of something we know from the Bible's book of Joshua, wherein the sun clearly revolves around the earth.

It's not such an outdated belief, after all. In a way, it's an impressively steadfast belief. Every few years, to the chagrin of every teacher who ever lived after Copernicus, a new poll comes out suggesting that when

---

10. The idea that Hollywood can more easily imagine the end of the world than an alternative to capitalism is a frequent theme in Žižek's work. On one of the more famous occasions, he proclaimed this among the protesters gathered with Occupy Wall Street in New York. See Žižek, "We Are Not Dreamers."

Americans are asked whether the sun goes around the earth or if the earth revolves around the sun, around one in four people get the answer wrong. The crazy thing about assuming the sun begins its revolution around the earth by rising every morning in the east is this: the sun really does rise in the east. Here is another example of believing what we plainly see, and it's a story of how all sacrifices began.

In the beginning, at the dawn of the agricultural age some ten thousand years ago, a Mesopotamian farmer arose before dawn. He set together a few stones, and he slaughtered one from his livestock upon the alter. The scent rose to the heavens, and it pleased the sun god. Every day he would rise to sacrifice to the sun god, and on most days the sun god did indeed arise. On occasion, the clouds obscured the sun god, and this told our farmer one of two things: either (1) the sun god was displeased with the sacrifice (meaning the sacrifice must be doubled tomorrow), or (2) a neighboring tribe was sacrificing to a different god. He couldn't know how the moody sun god felt, so he could only conclude by playing it safe. He might go to war against the neighbor and kill them all, and he would certainly make sure his children always rose before dawn to honor the sun god.

We learned to honor our gods like parents, because it worked out better for us. As the saying goes, God created humankind in God's image, and then humankind returned the favor. We engaged in sacrificial magic, because magic does indeed appear to work. Whether or not the sun shone upon our crops was no trivial matter. The difference of flourishing and starvation hung in the balance. The outsider who sacrificed to the cloud god was a threat to our physical survival, as was anyone in the community who dared rebel against the sun god. The gods were always angry, or at the very least they were always on the edge of wrath. The gods were moody as we are moody, for we forged the gods after our own image. If it were a relationship between two spouses, we'd call it co-dependent at best, abusive at worst. But like the tragedy of an abusive relationship where the mood is always unpredictable, we set out to please the gods who watched over us as warriors.

We would worship this god even in the midst of great tribulation, and perhaps we haven't evolved as much as we'd imagine. Let's switch from the Renaissance-era debate over geocentricism to today's debate about the end of the world. It's a debate between the apocalypse of God's tribulation and the apocalypse of climate change. If we began by worshiping the fire of the sun, it is a cruel irony that so many *do* in fact wish the world to end with heavenly fires of tribulation. Many wish for the day when God proves them right with the destruction of all evildoers. The desire for retributive punishment allows us to plummet ever closer to our true end, a heat not from heaven but from carbon. One in four of us answer that the sun goes round the earth, which is not to say a single person truly, deeply believes it. It was different in the days of Copernicus and Galileo, who lived in an age where people could point to the sky and then to a Bible and explain the text, clear as any day, plainly teaches geocentricism. History may play out similar themes, but it does not simply repeat itself. Our geocentricism today is a case of mistaken identity, a slip in the face of a smug pollster's "gotcha!" question, a half-belief which is never defended when pressed, but similarly outlandish polls cannot be so easily dismissed. This is how the world will end.

Almost half of the Christians in the United States—47 percent—tell the pollster they believe the world will end by 2050.[11] Half of Christians in the United States, or about one in three citizens overall, is a rather large number, is it not? Among white Evangelicals, the number is 58 percent. The phenomenon also negatively correlates with education. Among those with no college experience, 59 percent expect Christ's return by 2050; among college graduates, the number stands at 19 percent. It's enough to scare children with tales of antichrists and end times, but it's also enough to de-rail global negotiations over climate change and warfare.

Is this belief is sustained by a wish? Unlike our story of Columbus, whose belief could be called both illusion and delusion, a perpetually postponed rapture and apocalypse can't be verified as true or false. We can't quite call it delusion no matter how certain we are it's delusional, because the disconfirming (non)event in the future is perpetually postponed. But can we can ask why so many desire the earth's annihilation? Disabusing ourselves of beliefs which are simply false is rarely difficult. If we really don't want the world to end, we might take steps to stop it—beginning with abandoning the expectation the world *must* end in the near future. But on the other hand, where men desire their enemy's destruction in holy fire, the delusional belief held aloft by a wish seems impossible to eradicate. We find the idea of a massive comet colliding with the planet infinitely more believable that a world where everyone's basic needs are provided for and poverty is eliminated. We have a death drive, and our creativity aims at

11. Pew Research Center, "Public Sees a Future Full of Promise and Peril." See also Pew Research Center, "U.S. Christians' Views on the Return of Christ."

self-destruction rather than the healing of the world. Here is the story of how the apocalypse became popular in American Christianity.

In the winter of 1827–1828, an Irish Anglican pastor named John Nelson Darby had a ferocious idea.[12] From the earliest days, the church scattered across the Roman Empire had been apocalyptic. It was only after the expected Christ never returned that the church began to organize itself and its sacred texts. The Bible taught of Christ returning in loud glory, and it taught of Christ returning as a quiet thief in the night. How could an event be both clandestine and unmistakably triumphant? How else to reconcile the contradiction, Darby thought, than to say the return was not merely one second coming but instead two? Thusly so, Darby gifted the world a new idea, a *second,* second arrival he called the rapture, which he said would precede the final coming of Christ. In this secret arrival, the Christ would take the righteous away into the skies of paradise. The world would then collapse under the wrath of God's judgment and the vicious rule of an antichrist, but the righteous wouldn't be there to feel the pains of death, persecution, and destruction. The idea is not yet 200 years old, but its effects are everywhere. It's a belief so popular that few Christians in the world haven't ever heard of it. How better to stifle the anxiety over death by suggesting we might not ever die? How better to mitigate our concern for the world (or justify its extermination) than to suggest the end approaches, but we'll no longer be here to suffer consequences?

It was a historical anomaly for the rapture to survive and flourish. It was part of a whole system Darby created where the biblical timeline was divided into seven dispensations, and the result was a theology now called Dispensationalism. Very few Evangelical churches in America today are left untouched by Dispensationalism's influence. Even in Darby's day, those in his church who were understandably doubtful about the creation of an extra, clandestine invasion by the Christ faced expulsion from the church. The rapture didn't spread well in Britain, but Darby's followers began to spread it with some small success in America. The turning point came in the first decade of the twentieth century, when the American fundamentalist movement picked up steam and argued there were certain things Christians must believe. The exact list of the fundamentals was contentious, but they eventually boiled down to (1) the virgin birth of Christ, (2) the literal

---

12. At least, this is when he later claimed to have discovered the rapture. He did not go public with the idea until a few years later, leading some to suggest he may have faked an earlier date in order to claim authority over others who were beginning to explore the idea around the same time.

resurrection of Christ, (3) the substitutionary atonement of Christ, (4) the literal inspiration of the Bible without any error, and (5) the historical happening of Christ's miracles (or according to another list, the second coming of Christ). Though the inerrancy of the Bible and the substitutionary atonement of Christ were not ideas with which the earliest churches would have been familiar, they were now the standard for a uniquely American version of Christianity. We write our history retroactively.

The spread of these ideas was not simply a matter of theology but instead a balance of power and cash. A group of wealthy businessmen, led by the oil tycoon brothers Milton and Lyman Stewart, helped the fundamentalist movement by pouring money into publishing houses, churches, seminaries, and missionary movements. The Stewarts were not entirely unlike the Koch brothers today, who discreetly pour money into fringe political causes that then appear to be popular, grassroots movements. The businessmen made the distribution of fundamentalist literature free to all, and they heavily subsidized the publication of a new study Bible.

A new study Bible was perhaps the most important novelty contributing to the spread of the rapture. A man named Cyrus Scofield had grown in love with Darby's Dispensationalism, and so naturally his Bible would support the new theology. It was a King James Version of the Bible with footnotes included on every page to explain the meaning of the text to the reader. In a footnote to First Thessalonians, which contains a verse about meeting our king in the skies, Scofield explained the king's arrival was a secret arrival of Christ. Thusly so, most Americans were exposed for the first time to the rapture. Today we have Bibles of every conceivable translation and for every particular study group, but in the early twentieth century, the *Scofield Reference Bible* emerged amidst a poverty of options available to the studious Christian. It was the Bible your grandparents and great grandparents read, and the end of the world was literally written into it as a footnote.

I joke with my students my home of Los Angeles has a history of accidentally recreating Christianity. The *Scofield Reference Bible* was produced there in 1909, as was much of the fundamentalist literature, but Los Angeles was also a birthplace of Pentecostalism after the Azusa Street Revival in 1906. It was the site of one of the first megachurches (Angelus Temple, led by Amiee Semple McPherson in the 1920s). The teaching from this church was responsible not only for popularizing the megachurch, influencing Hollywood culture, and incorporating Hollywood thematics into church popularization (McPherson used airplanes and motorcycles as stage props for messages), but it also played an important role in the Christian rejection of Darwinism (which was not initially interpreted as an unacceptable belief for conservative Christians). Further, America at large and Los Angeles in particular were the base for massive missionary activity in this era, so whatever happened here spread across the globe in short order. Thusly so, American Evangelicalism is now synonymous with the megachurch, Pentecostalism makes up a quarter of Christians worldwide, the rapture is seen as a perfectly normal belief, and nearly half of American Christians expect the world to end by 2050.[13] By the time Evangelicalism was reinvented in the 1980s as a distinctly conservative, political cause organized by the Religious Right, it had all the tools it needed to ignore the climate collapse first detected in the same decade.

There is irony all around. Recall again the saying we mentioned before—God created us after God's image, and then we returned the favor. Consider the dismissive tone many in the American South take toward Hollywood without realizing that, in a very real sense, Los Angeles created the South's religion. But the cruelest irony is this: a religious movement originally fueled by oil money led us to the cliff's edge today, where we no longer care if the world is being heated beyond repair. Oil money converted into theology, which converted back into an almost theological trust in oil. The oil warned us of an apocalypse, and we returned the favor by inviting its aid in our demise.

I was raised in the one-third of America where the rapture was assumed as normal teaching, and this is the story of how this belief ceased working for me. I was speaking with a pastor whose world depended on destruction—the rapture, the final approval of God, and the damnation of the different—and I asked something simple. This was the same character of whom I spoke in our first chapter, the one who said caring for the poor would be a ridiculous waste of resources. His thinking always had a remarkable consistency to it. Whereas many Evangelicals would run from the darker implications of their faith, his embrace of those elements helped me see the dangerous fault lines. The exact conversation has long since escaped my memory, but it was a question about why his church didn't promote the care for creation. His answer had his characteristically coherent logic: "If God is going to destroy the world soon, why should we take care of it even

13. To clarify, I am not claiming all those who expect apocalypse also believe uniformly about the rapture. I know of no survey that has investigated the matter so closely. It would be more accurate to suggest premillennialism and the rapture provide fertile ground for less specific doomsday thinking. Beliefs always hide among others.

if we believed the climate scientists?" He believed we would be effectively working *against* God if we recycled. Rather than critique his logic, I claim such a cold answer reflects the only ultimately honest path for those who need destruction. His beliefs were sustained by a wish with abusive and horrific conclusions. I want to argue that we actually do need to chase down those horrific flaws if we are not to hide our eyes from the brutal implications of our ideologies and theologies. His logic was not an aberration. Brutality is a primary feature of the Evangelical system; it isn't a bug.

Darby was consistent, and consistency requires creativity. One of the themes we explore in this book the split between primary beliefs that then require us to derive secondary beliefs. In the same way that whatever we repress by day will return to haunt our dreams by night, it is often the secondary beliefs—which we only hold onto for the support of another idea—that cause us the most trouble. Whatever doesn't work is what always needs our attention. Even though one in three Americans claim to believe the world will end in three or four decades, we know the belief enters and escapes at will. Of course, the same one-third of Americans still invests in retirement plans. Belief is consistent when it suits, but belief is happy to throw off its mask and escape when it's unwelcome. When do beliefs escape? When do they stop inflicting themselves upon us?

I Know, but Does the Big Other Know?

There is a joke famous among psychoanalysts to show our dependence on belief in the third person, or through a proxy. It's unlikely there is even a single person alive who doesn't know what it means to depend on another's belief; indeed, your very act of deciding this book is worth reading depends on the expectation I might have something to say. Likewise, every child looks up to a parent trusting the parent to know, and part of maturity is realizing our parents (like ourselves) were only doing the best they knew how—no parent really knows as much as the child assumes. The reverse is also true, for when a child stops believing in Santa Claus, it is the parent—not the child—that experiences the trauma of disbelief. The shock comes from realizing the holidays will have less magic after the loss of belief, and the parent knows more changes are just around the corner. What these examples tell us is belief in the third person (via another who is supposed to believe for us) is a natural, even unavoidable human phenomenon. Once more, it is not the delusional belief itself which is so difficult to disabuse ourselves of and rid from our psyche. Instead, it's the delusional belief sustained by a wish that will remain in place without considering the evidence to the contrary. It's the vicious delusion-illusion hybrid lurking beneath the surface and it plagues us. Our story of belief in the third person begins in a psychiatric ward.

This is the story from the psychoanalysts about belief in the third person. A man suffered intense trauma and descended into schizophrenia. He was paralyzed with the psychotic idea that he was a piece of seed on the ground, immobile and vulnerable, lying there to be trampled. After many years, the psychiatrists were able to convince him of his delusion. He claimed to be cured. "This is wonderful—I'm a human being, I'm freed!" He told his psychiatrists. But they weren't yet convinced.

The psychiatrists set a final test for the supposedly cured psychotic. As the man walked out to the entryway of the clinic, he shrieked in fear. He ran back to the ward and screamed of how someone had left a chicken at the door outside. "It's going to eat me!"

"We've been over this a thousand times," they told him. "You are freed. You are a human being, not a seed to be trampled or eaten."

"Of course I know this—but does the chicken know?"

We might laugh away such a ridiculous joke, but the terrible truth is that it captures so much of our frantic activity. We may (consciously) know our priest has all the same doubts we have. We may know our politicians don't have the answers they promise. We may know our parents are not judging us. We may know the child on the playground who ridiculed us didn't really mean much (and likely doesn't remember). We supposedly know so many things about what we should or shouldn't concern ourselves. Nevertheless, since when did knowing anything matter all that much? We know the cruel joke from childhood meant nothing, but the teasing lives on in our memories. We may know those dysfunctional relationships of the past no longer define us, we may know the gods are dead, and we may know we are not a piece of seed on the ground—but does the big Other know?

Again, when the child stops believing in Santa Claus, it is the parents who have all the anxiety. "What will become of the fun we had in the holiday traditions?" they ask, and, "What other changes are right around the corner for the child growing up?" In the same way the parents experience the anxiety at the lost belief of the child, we tend to invest trust and enjoyment circuitously. We believe in the third person. We believe on the condition someone else believes for us.

Examples of this belief in the third person, through proxy stand-ins, are everywhere. Those concerned with our culture's supposed increasing acceptance of sexual permissiveness are sure some nebulous hedonist is experiencing all the pleasure they wish they had, which they cannot admit they desire. The parent who does not want to visit his own parents will tell a daughter she should want to visit grandma. We are not sure we are loved, so we demand our significant other demonstrate unconditional love to prove ourselves acceptable. The parishioner in the church pews does not believe in God this week, but at least the priest believes. Or the Eucharist believes. Or the songs and official statements believe. This is belief in the third person. It is toxic, dishonest, and altogether ridiculous; it is also entirely human.

Occasionally there are those who claim they have left the religion of their youth behind and have ventured on into the atheist terrain. What interests me, however, is how so many will turn around to me, someone who did not ask to be in this position, and ask one final question about the possibility their soul could end up in hell. Or they ask why their (former) pastor never explained how we have 5,300 ancient Greek manuscripts of the New Testament but not one of them match any other. The questions are fairly standard along the lines of science, sexuality, or occasionally history. Why someone who ostensibly no longer believes should still ask about theology doesn't even cross their mind. It's as if belief entrenches itself into our psyches in a way that can't be entirely undone.

There are philosophers who say, in our supposedly secularist, postmodern, and anti-religious times, that we actually believe now more than ever. It's merely the sources of authority that changed. Žižek put it this way: "Belief is a notion that displays the deadlock characteristic of the Real: on the one hand, nobody can fully assume belief in the first person singular . . . . On the other hand, however, no one really escapes belief—a feature that deserves to be emphasized especially today, in our allegedly godless times."[14] No matter how supposedly secular we become, we still summon the gods in a different guise. We have an inability to risk faith in ourselves and accept responsibility for the horrifying conclusion that our beliefs are unfounded, untethered, and indefensible. We no longer believe in the first person; we now believe through proxies. We believe, because we must. We didn't ask for it, and we won't escape it. We will get the proxy we deserve, who we will pay to speak the words our itching ears desire to hear.

14. Žižek, *Did Somebody Say Totalitarianism?*, 88.

Diogenes the Great

Upon entering the city and catching sight of the rumored madman, the emperor introduced himself: "I am Alexander the Great."

The dog replied, "And I! I am Diogenes the Cynic." The emperor of the world—who didn't yet know his conquests would come to ruin when his generals divided up his empire after his death—was shocked at so little reverence. He wondered if Diogenes was not afraid of his power.

"Should I be afraid of you? Do you consider yourself a good man or a bad man?" the irreverent dog asked before continuing, "I myself am not a man at all but instead a dog who bites. Do you know what is worse than a dog who bites?—A man who flatters."

"I can see your lack of flattery has taken you so very far in life. You say people give to beggars, but not to philosophers, because people think they might become poor while nobody fears a lapse into thinking. How many friends has this attitude procured?" Alexander hadn't ever encountered one who didn't fear his might, but he was beginning to like the character.

"I'm rightly accused. Now tell me, my good man, what will you do with your day while I lie here?"

"I suppose I should conquer the rest of the Greeks," Alexander began. Diogenes asked what he would do after he tired of the Greeks. "I suppose I should then go on to conquer Asia." Diogenes agreed and again asked what next. "I suppose it would be best to conquer the entire world." And then? "Well, if I have the whole world, I could then relax at my palace."

"Indeed you could, but isn't this the whole difference between me and Alexander the Great?" smirked the dog. "Diogenes the Great prefers to skip the conquering portion of his schedule and relax today."

6 The Cynic and the Fool

In the summer of 1520, Pope Leo X issued a papal bull demanding Martin Luther recant everything he'd taught. Luther had grown furious over the sale of indulgences, which were being used to enrich the Vatican's accounts and construct ever more elaborate buildings. Indulgences rendered salvation into an economic exchange. A small sum of money now could cut short time in purgatory later. You wouldn't want to imagine meeting your grandfather in purgatory only to be asked while you hadn't handed over a little cash to spare him centuries of angst before entering paradise. Luther's rage was stoked by the realization his flock of mostly illiterate German peasants were being taken advantage of by the priests, as those priests knew the peasants hadn't enough education to recognize the whole practice as a contrived money-making scheme rather than a biblical practice. After Luther posted his Ninety-five Theses in 1517 in response to this abusive practice, the Church had sought to quietly work through back channels via scholarly disputes. By 1520, the Holy Roman Empire was beginning to fracture, and along with it the Church's authority had escaped. The pope didn't know what Luther knew.

Only a few months before the pope demanded recantation, Luther discovered a book by Lorenzo Valla.[1] The book attacked a single document called "The Donation of Constantine," which claimed the Roman Emperor Constantine gave an ancient pope control over all of Western Europe. The Vatican used this one document to exert secular authority for centuries, and Valla's book proved the document was a forgery. After reading of

1. See Whitford, "The Papal Antichrist."

forgery, Luther had all the evidence he needed to say the Church was a liar overcome with greed and aspirations of power, qualities defining an antichrist in the New Testament. Luther didn't know whether anyone alive at the Vatican knew of the forgery, but Luther was certain all of Europe had been fooled by the charlatan. If he was going to be threatened with excommunication, he'd gladly leave. A few months later, shortly before Christmas, Luther gathered his followers together in the city square and burned the papal bull. In the first week of January 1521, he was excommunicated. Like a dysfunctional relationship, it is sometimes when we no longer have the choice to go back that we are most free.

When we encounter a claim which cannot possibly be true, the most important question we must ask ourselves is whether the claim pours out of the heart of a cynic or a fool. Lest it seem a novel idea of my own to write a book on cynics and fools, we must consider whether we ever go a day in our lives without swimming through a ocean of con artists and charlatans. We call them politicians and priests, and occasionally we call them friends and coworkers. The cynic and the fool fill our media streams and our wandering thoughts, for every time we hear a claim which cannot possibly be true, our question is always the same: (1) is this person a *fool* who really believes in the words proceeding from the mouth, or (2) does this manipulative *cynic* know exactly what they are doing with the fib?

Cynicism can be a positive and healthy thing, and indeed there is a heroic bravery or realism in recognizing our leaders might have concealed interests. As we said in the first chapter, cynicism can be a positive and healthy skepticism, or it can be a manipulative and nihilistic opportunism. I am aiming against the manipulative version, which is often found in the politician who is called cynical; when we say a politician is cynical, we are not speaking of her brave skepticism so much as her will-to-power at all costs. We'd be speaking of one who saw the defenseless as means to an end, namely, power. What might have begun as healthy, skeptical cynicism can, over time, turn into a negative cynicism that is more like the role of the knave who does nothing but lie and manipulate. Whether the cynic is positive or negative, the fool won't recognize any of it. Whether out of honesty or ignorance, the fool merely wants to believe directly.

Radicals Always Short-Circuit the Truth

In the book of Isaiah, God commissioned the prophet to speak to Israel with a piercingly sarcastic and deeply solemn message:

> Be ever hearing but never understanding;
>   Be ever seeing, but never perceiving.
> Make the heart of this people calloused;
>   Make their ears dull
>   and close their eyes.
> Otherwise they might see with their eyes,
>   hear with their ears,
>   understand with their hearts,
>   and turn and be healed.[2]

The prophet asked how long he should speak, and the voice of a big Other commanded the prophet to stay silent until the cities laid in ruins and the land in waste. The voice said only a stump of a great tree would survive the ominous fires engulfing the countryside. There is a lesson here: rather than warn the people with trumpets, a prophet always speaks a message with too few words.

Parables and jokes always deploy such brevity. Consider the way a joke functions; it succeeds precisely by saying too little and leaving us to fill in the gaps. We enjoy the joke when it goes beyond our expectations into the domain of the unexpected, into the genuinely new, and into the surprise of a wrong turn. A joke merely giving the answer we were expecting isn't much of a joke. There is something about a joke that triggers our pleasure in being *in* on the missing information. Likewise, if we ask a question and receive the answer we were expecting, was it really a question?

There's a joke Freud loved wherein two men became extremely wealthy in their business dealings and yet remain unhappy. They had all the funds to live comfortably with their millions, but the elites with old family money wouldn't accept them as equals. So to win the approval of their rich peers, they began their social climb by commissioning a famous artist to paint their portraits. When they hosted a dinner party to celebrate the unveiling of the portraits, the city's curious aristocrats came, wondering what had become of the two ambitious men. The only problem was they invited a celebrated art critic as well. The critic was less impressed than they had hoped, for the critic noticed a rather important figure was missing, which

2. Isa 6:9–10 (NIV).

should have been painted to hang in between the two. The critic shames them with a question: *"But where is the savior?"*[3]

What is happening in this joke at the businessmen's expense? We might recall Saint Jerome, who claimed every rich man is either a thief or else the son of a thief. Or we might simply recall our Gospels, where a savior says a camel will squeeze itself through the eye of a needle before a rich man can enter the kingdom of God. At any rate, the joke only works if we realize the critic was likening the two entrepreneurs to two thieves hanging beside Christ on the cross. The art critic's snark was a sharp rebuttal, but it was not a well-planned critique of wealth and power. It worked precisely by saying too few words.

A joke is a short circuit toward the truth, cutting across several ideas that wouldn't usually go together. To tell a joke, to prophesy to a people, to tell a parable, or to be a public thinker and leader today requires we follow this same circuitous path to the truth. We needn't speak every thought filling our heads; we need only say enough to trigger what the public already knows—though the knowledge is repressed. A joke succeeds in laughter from people already in on the information omitted, and it fails when told among a crowd not in on it. Likewise, theology should speak indirectly like a joke, triggering truths we already know and yet repress. Our task is to bring out into the open what lies beneath the surface of every conversation.

Those who prefer to manipulate and play upon the biases lurking beneath the surface are those we call cynics. Those who believe we might bring knowledge out into the open are those we call fools. If it is not clear, I am on the side of the fool, because any worthwhile philosophy aims to liberate the mind from enslavement.

We now dive into the mind of those who speak without regard for the rightness or wrongness of words. We will think about the complex and interlocking motives among groups of people—all of which we would diagnose differently on a spectrum of cynicism to foolishness or skepticism to literalism—who all interact with the same set of symbols and beliefs. If I say "I believe X," and you say "I believe X" as well, we haven't any guarantee the X means the same thing to each of us. Whole groups can appreciate a doctrine or symbol even if it means something entirely different to each person. What happens when we, like the fundamentalists, all depend on the same statement of faith even though we all mean different things by it?

---

3. Freud, *Jokes and Their Relation to the Unconscious*, 74.

When discussing the unconscious motives of another, the temptation is to hope we understand. But what any psychoanalyst would tell us is we must actually guard against understanding too much. There is more going on than meets the ears. To understand too much would mean we are interpreting meanings that aren't actually there. Our confirmation biases beg us to see meaning where there is none and agreement where there is dissension. So perhaps we should say it is actually by *refusing to understand* that we truly enter a new mode of understanding. By refusing to understand, we gain eyes to see and ears to hear.

There is a famous example of this need to refuse understanding from a 1938 issue of *Home and Garden* magazine.[4] It was written well before the horrors of Auschwitz were birthed, for the magazine article tells us of a benevolent Adolf Hitler who built himself a wondrous estate. His beautiful mountainside home was perched near a village, and Hitler had his chef bake pastries so he could pass treats out among the children. Hitler took daily strolls through his gardens and hatched scenic plans with his grounds keeper. His dogs ran free about the complex. Though Hitler was a vegetarian (indeed, he said he couldn't hurt a fly) his chef provided choice meats for his guests. Similarly, while Hitler wouldn't touch tobacco or alcohol (so moral was he) the estate has its own cigar chamber and wine cellar for guests who indulged in vice. The article celebrated his watercolor paintings and his personal library, and it tells us Hitler was a noble thinker, a storyteller, a reader, an artist, and a connoisseur.

Reading the article confronts me with a starkly troubling reality. I would likely have enjoyed the company of Hitler the artist, Hitler the reader, Hitler the kind man. Should I have found myself a guest at his mountain home, I would have listened to his stories and dry humor, and I would have laughed with my gracious host. I might have said of him what we often say of those with a horrific, dark side: if only you got to know him, you would like him. What we must realize instead is the truth of Hitler was not his mountain home but his Auschwitz. The truth of Hitler was not peace but war, and it is sometimes only by refusing to know the idealized side that we push the door open into truth. The racist always tells us they mean well, as does the misogynist, the fundamentalist, and all who do harm to others. There's always an excuse, and nobody thinks of herself as an irrational

---

4. The article surfaced nearly fifteen years ago and was republished in the *Guardian*. A fight over copyrights resulted in its being scrubbed from the Internet, but if you so desire, search for the 1938 *Home and Garden* article "Hitler's Mountain Home."

bigot. We must guard against understanding too much, because occasionally understanding too much (or justifying too much) is precisely what closes our eyes and ears.

What follows is indebted to the theory of the psychoanalyst Jacques Lacan.[5] He was speaking of politics when he noticed the Left operates according to a logic of foolishness while the Right operates according to a logic of cynicism. And though we might detect his biases with regard to political persuasion, we can see a strong undercurrent operating just as clearly in our religious domains. One caveat: do not assume all sides are equally wrong just because both sides have flaws. I don't want to appear to equivocate as if I am indifferent and criticize everyone equally, for the commonplace line "both sides have a point" and its variants are all too often an excuse for poor thinking. The human drive to mis-recognize and terrorize is an insatiable beast, and not all ideologies are created equal.

Foolishness of the Left

True believers on both the Left and the Right depend on direct belief. For example, the Christian or Muslim fundamentalist does not say she *thinks* such-and-such is true; no, instead she *knows*. As the philosopher Søren Kierkegaard taught, the only type of faith to truly merit the name faith is always paradoxical. If it can be shown reasonable, no faith is necessary. It's true of theology, it's true of all abstract theory, and it's true of all the basic assumptions guiding our lives. We may know, for example, the chances of a marriage working are only one in two, but love puts this knowledge aside. Love both knows and, paradoxically, chooses not to know. This paradox is precisely what the Christian or Muslim fundamentalist cannot have. Wherever we know without doubt, we haven't room left for faith. But we are a species imagining we desire knowledge without doubt, so we claim we know directly. How then do our leaders engage our desire to trust in a subject-supposed-to-know?

The Leftist organizer generally operates with direct belief. The Leftist directly believes in the causes she promotes, but she has a posture of insecurity attached to this confidence. For example, we needn't really wonder whether a progressive politician is being paid off to support health care, immigration reform, or rights for minorities. We needn't wonder why the liberal priest supports the inclusion of those who traditionalists prefer to

5. See Lacan, *The Ethics of Psychoanalysis*, 182–83.

keep out of a congregation. We needn't wonder why the college student spends hours in the sun collecting signatures for a cause such as higher pay or student loan reform. There are certainly a great number of causes people support for questionable, hidden reasons, but there are also many causes pure enough (or even self-detrimental enough) that we can assume authenticity.

The psychoanalysts teach us there are people who both (1) desire to be the object of affection of their romantic partner while they also (2) feel terrified their partner would be fully satisfied in the relationship. Why might this be? The fear stems from the expecting if the Other is truly satisfied, then the we're no longer necessary. Some find it easier to prop up desire by sabotaging both the Other's satisfaction. This of course means the relationship is always unstable. The partner might say "I want what is best for each of us," but unconsciously the desire is for just enough dissatisfaction for the game to continue.

The Left deploys this strategy of provocation by making demands it knows won't be met, and it does so in hopes the demands will stir new possibilities. There's an famous clinical case study illuminating this desire in which a girl named Anna O. seemed to accidentally sabotage her analyst and, as a result, sabotage her own progress as well.[6] Anna came from a family described as puritanical, and her life was monotonous. As a way to enliven her days, Anna systematically daydreamed what she called a "private theater." Her symptoms became so great that she lost the ability to speak at times, and she experienced overwhelming anxiety and what she called "absences," during which she would hallucinate. She needed to tell her analyst (Josef Breuer) all of her stories and hallucinations in order for her symptoms to subside. Once again, just as we often reveal what most preoccupies us precisely by not speaking, we may also conceal our truth by speaking too much.

Anna began doing something we so rarely see in either the clinic or in ordinary conversation; she vocally divided her sessions into two terms: (1) the serious work of the "talking cure" and (2) the laughably pessimistic "chimney sweeping." Both were ways of describing the same talking cure, and she alluded to chimney sweeping only as a joke, but in my interpretation the term also betrayed doubts as to whether she could ever come clean. She was regularly obstinate with her analyst, who had to coax her to share her stories. She unconsciously sabotaged her progress and seemed to act

6. See Breuer, "Anna O.," 60–78.

as if resolving her hallucinations would also put an end to the energy motivating her behavior. Her family was paying for both the effective and the
ineffective sessions, but she seemed perfectly content to waste their money
and her time by playing this perpetual game of storytelling as she recounted
her private theater. Chimney sweeping was a curious term to select. When
one sweeps a chimney, a great deal of soot stirs up without anything getting
entirely clean. It will be filled with ash again in no time. We could think of
chimney sweeping as a talking cure (an effort to sort through our issues),
or instead we could point to how we, at all costs, avoid realizing how we
merely repeat our symptoms and daydreams. We'd rather avoid recognizing the reasons hiding underneath our mundane conversations, arguments,
and dreams. It doesn't get us anywhere, but we stir up a great deal of soot
in the process .

Anna's fear was of loosing energy by talking away her symptom, but
don't we so very often fear resolution precisely because resolving a problem
will bring us into unfamiliar terrain? The Leftist voice stirs up a great deal
of causes. Whether we judge them good or bad, it doesn't take much effort
for us to recognize them as genuinely felt. But just as Anna stabilized her
reality by keeping things from changing too much (in her case, by perpetually telling stories from her own private theater), the progressive politician offers up a variety of causes that they very well believe in (full access
to healthcare, rights for minorities, higher wages, etc.) while sometimes
ignoring the rational conclusions of their theory. That conclusion might
implicate neoliberal capitalism as a whole rather than merely critiquing its
excessive abuses. While we do not have a Leftist party at this moment in
American history, we see this avoidance in the liberal party in each election
cycle. At least since the Supreme Court's Citizens United decision, which
allowed unlimited corporate money to influence the outcome of elections,
we see only disinterested muttering on the troubles of money in politics.
We hear the chimney sweeping of important causes with badly needed
resolution, but we don't expect to hear much about campaign finance. We
hear disingenuous lament over the abusive excesses of capitalism, but we
seem to never talk about the fact that, within capitalism, nobody is ever
paid for the full value of their work; if we were, there would be no profit to
extract from a laborer and reallocate to an owner.

Let's take the example of the liberal pundit on cable news. The pundit desires to directly (foolishly, if authentically) believe in a position even
though his desire is always thwarted. When he interviews a guest with

extreme, ideological views and no qualms with brandishing an outlandish ideology, how does the liberal pundit respond? There is always a choice of whether to treat extremists as if they either (1) actually believe their own rhetoric or (2) merely pretend to hold a view to hide ulterior motives. The first path insults the extremist's intelligence, while the second path insults the extremist's morality. In fact, when watching these interactions in the real time of live television, we can even see the pundit hesitate as he tries to decide which insulting path to take. Sometimes it is easiest to let the lie go unnamed, because figuring out someone's motives is difficult.

Indeed, upon hearing an absurd claim, we're often confronted with exactly this conundrum. One the one hand, we can reply, "Well, have you considered the horror of your beliefs if taken to their rational conclusion?" Or on the other hand, in a manner ironically recalling the famous conservative pundit William F. Buckley's standard line, we may retort, "I will not insult your intelligence by treating you as if you are as stupid as you pretend to be." This choice is a bit humorous to watch the liberal pundit make in real time, for the reflective person is always on an edge of chaos. Those of us who think ourselves intellectuals inhabit a world of self-doubt, and the position of the pundit is always unsure.

The Left plays the role of the self-saboteur in a relationship, and it balances this position with the possibility of progress. The self-saboteur has the intuition and knows all is not well, and the self-saboteur pokes at the Other to keep the game in motion. It places demands upon the body politic that it will never fulfill, however rational or workable they might be. But if we are in a relationship where we are always prodding and demanding, always looking for a guarantee we are one step ahead of the Other, we cannot truly communicate. I do not say this to denigrate the Left, for communication isn't necessarily a virtue when communication requires us to pretend certain extremist viewpoints are authentic. Those who say "both sides have a point" will doubtlessly call me dismissive or divisive, but I don't want to live in a society where certain horrific ideas are considered legitimate options.

What Anna called chimney sweeping in the one-on-one clinical setting, Žižek calls a "staged theater" in politics: things change just enough so that everything remains basically the same.[7] Society would revolt if a candidate told us outright she planned to dream small and make only the slightest adjustments. Or perhaps the horrific truth is we would applaud. If

---

7. Žižek, "Paul and the Truth Event," 85.

we repeatedly made the exact same mistake and yield the same results, the problem would be easy to identify. It's necessary to adjust our mistakes just enough so we never see repetition as repetition. Alcoholics Anonymous famously defines insanity as endless repetition with the expectation of new results. Recall the famous saying that those who dare not remember history are doomed to repeat it; it isn't quite the case we simply don't remember, but instead we do everything in our power to misremember. We aren't so clever at identifying the causes underneath the symptoms, so we change just enough so things might remain basically the same. Repetition of the old way demands novelty—not the altogether new, but just enough new-ness so we may trick ourselves into thinking something is new. And we will cheer and vote to keep the monstrous machine in motion.

Cynicism of the Right

There are (at least) two sides to every story. If the left-wing leader desires to play the part of the fool, Lacan described the logic of the Right in a remarkably different way. And whether or not we agree with his obvious biases (for these figures of cynics and fools clearly manifest along every point of the political spectrum), we can see a theme of different relationships to belief shaping the contours of every ideology, whether cultural, religious, political, or even scientific. Put simply, the ultra-conservative ideologue knows the role he is expected to play.

So to examine the role of the cynic, let's suppose a journalist attends a rally for an ambitious figure mounting a presidential campaign.[8] Let us further suppose this figure comes from a wealthy family with vast resources, he attended an elite university and studied abroad, and he has friends all over the world and finds no difficulty in winning over people from diverse backgrounds. He now finds himself in a rural community holding a rally for people who value their traditions and take pride in their heritage. We can imagine strong family ties in this community keep the graduating high school seniors close to home, and we can imagine family, tradition, and faith play a crucial role in tying the community together. They hope the

---

8. For the record, I wrote this example before a certain business mogul, who shall not be named, declared his 2016 presidential campaign. In fact, this is loosely adapted from an example Lacan created back in 1960. In my estimation, the mogul not a brilliantly calculating knave so much as he is a fool. More precisely, he is a narcissist first, a fool second, and a cynical con man third. We should interpret his actions in that order.

world never changes from the world in which they were raised, and they lament that so much has been done to undermine their familiar world.

In order to identify with those in the crowd, the politician speaks of the ills of the east coast Washington elite. He decries the massive influx of immigrants bearing little regard for traditional American customs. He demands we ban those who don't share our faith. He speaks boldly of our need to maintain American supremacy and military might, and he laments the government regulation that supposedly decimated the job market. All of these ills, he tells the cheering crowd, will be rectified, and the day is coming when America no longer tolerates the out-of-touch elite who look down upon tightly knit communities. There is applause and laughter. Resentments are triggered and hope is stoked. Our candidate needn't stretch far for examples of what the crowd will hate, for in a very real sense, he merely describes his own upbringing as everything wrong with the nation. He essentially describes himself while framing himself as a man of the people, the protector of the blue collar. Most importantly, he frames his talk so the audience never notices he was describing himself. Nostalgia is such an effective tool for a society obsessed with imaginary pasts.[9]

After the rallying crowds have left, our journalist finds the politician sitting at the hotel's bar reading over his poll numbers and schedule for the following day. With no small amount of fear and trepidation, the journalist approaches the candidate to ask: "Did your speech really reflect how you see the world? I wonder how a man of your stature, with your education and experience, could say so many negative things about those struggling to survive—do you really believe all this?"

The charlatan sets his papers down and smiles. "Come now, do you understand so little? Don't insult my intelligence and suggest I'm so very backwards. I am just doing what they pay me to do!"

All this rage must be preached to cheering masses, for as the philosopher Michel Foucault used to say, the masses have a curious desire

9. Wherever I use the idea of nostalgia for an imaginary past, I am indebted to McGowan, *Enjoying What We Don't Have*. This nostalgia is a powerful tool within populist politics and religion alike, as it indicates a false belief in a better world that we should ostensibly return to even though it never existed. For example, the idealized moral order of the 1950s included massive doses of racism, its sexual permissiveness was statistically identical to today (though seldom discussed openly), and its economic prosperity was due to post-war negotiations that might have worked well for the suburbs but were disastrous elsewhere. It was not a uniquely "great" time but instead an era easily misremembered. Nevertheless, it has been a tradition since time immemorial to label the newest generation as somehow worse than the ones before.

for fascism.[10] It was true when a very clever Hitler took power of a nation where Christianity comprised more than 95 percent of the population, and, no less, he did it by stoking the prized values of patriotism and traditional family values. It was true then, and it isn't as if we evolved past that desire for fascism in the few years since. What this story of the journalist and the candidate suggests is not merely the cynicism of hypocrisy. The political charlatan actively believes his cynical ends (election) justify the means (using his constituent's biases against them). Rather than seeing himself as a hypocrite, he genuinely believes this is the game we are demanding he play. And he is right.

I would argue this dynamic, where the cynic acts as if hypocrisy itself is type of virtuous morality, is why our culture became so fascinated with the Netflix series *House of Cards*. Frank Underwood (Kevin Spacey) is ruthless in his rise from House Majority Whip to President. He, along with his wife Claire Underwood (Robin Wright), initially appear to be in a symbiotic relationship held together by pure ambition.

The sexual affairs in which each engage, though normally a plot device to drive a couple apart, are ingeniously deployed by the series's writers to show that a bond of unquestionable commitment exists between the two. The commitment transcends their material existence, their lack of satisfaction in each other, and a pervasive sense of emptiness. This unquestionable commitment is revealed early in the series when Frank Underwood approaches Claire's affair. Her lover falsely believes Claire will leave her husband to carry on the affair with him. Without any trace of fear, Frank Underwood tells the lover he couldn't possibly comprehend how little he matters to her. We find out the various affairs they engage in are authorized by a long-standing agreement between the two of them. The couple is held together by an ideal of unstoppable power, and ideals are not destroyed by preauthorized sexual transgressions. The drive to power is singular and unstoppable, and it matters not who is harmed in the process. Still this does not keep others from working with him and even finding his methods enviable.

In the first season, Frank Underwood befriends a struggling alcoholic congressman and a young, ambitious journalist. Each feels they have something to gain from a liaison with the cynical Underwood, and each are destroyed as they become obstacles to his rise. Every person who becomes an obstacle is destroyed with the exception of Underwood's Chief of Staff

10. Foucault, *Power/Knowledge*, 139.

Doug Stamper (Michael Kelly), whose failings of addiction and violence are forgiven because they're the inevitable conclusion of his unshakable commitment to Underwood's rise. Every system of ideology does exactly this: it either implicitly authorizes transgression or even explicitly requires betrayal.

Those who are obstacles to the Underwoods' rise are expendable, and we see no conflict between the Underwoods and their coconspirators until the precise moment when someone begins to directly believe in an ethical or political cause. The chief of sins for the cynic is that somebody would truly believe. The cynic must expel the fool.

In later seasons, we even see the relationship between Frank and Claire Underwood fray for the same reason their relationships failed with everyone else, namely, she begins to care. In a very human story, these two arch-cynics are revealed as deeply insecure. They are merely shells of human beings with no real friends and a loveless relationship. Their outward success directly drains everything inside. Throughout *House of Cards*, the drive to the top sustained their relationship. With nowhere else to rise for President Underwood, and with no clear indication Claire Underwood will rise above her position as a UN ambassador or Vice President, there is nowhere left to go but down into history. The couple achieved everything they desired, which has the effect of stopping the drive behind the motions.

Collectives: The Desire of Fools for Cynics and the Desire of Cynics for Fools

There is a story in which a man entered the home of the famous scientist Niels Bohr and saw a horseshoe hanging about the doorframe. Knowing a horseshoe is considered a good luck charm, the visitor felt astonished such a rational man could believe in such folklore. "Why, don't tell me you of all people buy into this nonsense!" he said.

Bohr replied, "No, no, of course I don't believe in it at all, but I'm told it works even if you don't believe."

So far we have only been exploring the cynic and the fool in political terms, but I suspect the analogues to religion are already apparent. So let's shift this discussion toward group dynamics bringing the spectrum of foolishness to cynicism into our everyday lives. As you doubtlessly know, it would be far too simplistic and entirely unrealistic to think each of us is either a cynic or a fool and nothing else. Every aspect of humanity exists along a spectrum, and this particular spectrum is no different. We use symbols as groups, and we understand them as individuals. At the individual level, the devastating differences emerge.

We said this spectrum of cynicism to foolishness is indebted to psychoanalyst Jacques Lacan, so we should take a look at another dynamic he explores: groups of fools seem to desire the leadership of a cynic. Concordantly, perhaps groups of cynics also desire a fool to lead them. Consider again the liberal Protestant congregation. Mainline liberal Christians often think of themselves as reasonable skeptics of the supernatural. They clearly see the tenants of the faith as significant, though they might hesitate at the idea of miracles. However skeptical they may be of the more fantastic claims of Christianity, they nevertheless desire a priest who truly and directly believes in the historic faith. No matter how skeptical (or even cynical) they may be about forgeries in the New Testament (for instance, the epistles bearing Saint Paul's name that were truly written much later), they still desire the priest to preach the Word of God each week. However doubtful they may feel about the story in book of Acts where the Holy Spirit causes the apostles to speak in foreign tongues, they still celebrate Pentecost as a high holy day. In short, even if they cannot bring themselves to believe, they desire another (person, or ritual) to believe for them.

The inverse is true of the conservative Christian. The Evangelical puts a high trust in the authority of their Scriptures, and they desire a leader who approaches the Bible with the same reverence. So they hire a pastor who will teach a consistent, straightforward reading of the Bible emphasizing it's perfection and trustworthiness as the Word of God. But if a minister did his assigned reading in seminary, he also knows—if no two of our 5,300 first-millennium Greek manuscripts are exactly alike—it is simply impossible to know exactly what an original text said. Even if his life depended on it, he knows he wouldn't be able to reconstruct even a single New Testament book with complete accuracy to the original, even before translating from Greek. Or perhaps (again, *if* he did his assigned reading in seminary) he knows parts of the Bible contradict each other—such as when the same battle is described in two books, but different numbers are given for the size of the army. Perhaps he is aware certain texts changed over time as official, orthodox theology changed. If the Bible was retranslated and changed to reflect a more original meaning (which is often done to reflect better understandings of terms related to gender, sexuality, eternity, etc.), it would be boycotted by Christians, so translators must bear the crude realities of marketability. The pastor of a conservative congregation is barred from mentioning any of this.

Perhaps this church naïvely assumes all Christians have always believed Christ paid the debt for our sins by substituting his death for our deserved punishment, but any well-read pastor knows Saint Anselm first articulated something approaching this view in 1098 CE.[11] Perhaps the people of this church only consider someone a Christian if we confess to having a personal relationship with Christ, but he knows we haven't much evidence of Christians using the phrase "personal relationship with Christ" until the late nineteenth century in America. In short, what options does a pastor have (after accumulating perhaps a hundred thousand dollars in student loans) when the congregation will only hire him if he suppresses almost everything he learned in seminary? Doesn't the message effectively become "Please lie to us!"? It seems we desire a leader who occupies a kind of inverse position to our belief; if we are insecure, we want a subject-supposed-to-know who embodies security. We'd never confess this, and we likely don't even recognize this desire, but this inverse logic lurks underneath the surface of modern Christianity.

Of course, this example only works if the pastor was indeed educated in his faith, and it is unfortunately common for education to be avoided in the first place. If we don't desire to know, then why invest in knowledge? If facts are not authoritative but instead relative, then why would a community desire a leader armed with facts? If we desire something to be true but find it difficult to believe, we might search out an article online verifying our perspective. We prefer an article loaded with data and statistics, and we expect it to cite books we will never read. All of this gives an air of authority, a position I cannot myself occupy and yet hope another may fulfill.

In the same way we have discussed belief in the proxy—an authority or a subject-supposed-to-know—we find belief in the third person is crucial to this cynic-fool spectrum. Žižek finds a traumatic example of this third-person belief in *Life Is Beautiful* (1997), a film about the Holocaust.[12] In the concentration camps, a father tells his son the horrors are all a mere game from which they will soon be released. This is clearly done to shield the child from the horror and almost certain death they face if the war continues. In fact, the father is also sustaining his hope indirectly through the son, for as long as the son thinks it's all a game the father too maintains

---

11. See Anselm, *Cur Deus Homo*.

12. See Žižek, *Did Somebody Say Totalitarianism?*, 68–73.

a plausible hope for release. The film concludes not long after the father's death, and even as he is led away to execution he winks to the son and continues to keep up the appearances of a game. Would not more interesting ending have been for the father to confess his fib, followed by the son responding, yes, he knew all along it wasn't a game but was merely pretending in order to shield his father from hopelessness? Had the film ended this way, it would have exemplified such a crucial thing we must understand about belief: nobody necessarily must believe directly so long as we suppose another to believe. We need only for the belief to appear plausible to another whose investment we trust. Believing through a subject-supposed-to-know—whether a father or a Father—is a curious human phenomenon.

In the example above of the pastor who must repress the vast majority of what he learned in seminary if he desires to keep a job, we noted a number of problems around understanding the biblical text. Those problems lead to a question: if anyone who has studiously examined the history of our tradition knows this, why isn't it spoken of? It would be easy to accuse the evasive pastor of cynicism, and to be sure, this is often the case, but it is equally true to say the congregation itself is the true collective cynic. The congregation may not realize what it's demanding when it expects adherence to a doctrinal statement, but if the choice is between the leader's honesty and joblessness on the one hand or white lies on the other, then who is to blame? Do we blame the pastor who chooses not to speak or the congregation that will not pay for honesty?

This dynamic of collectively foolish desire for a cynical leader is found within more dogmatic, conservative groups. So where do we find the find the opposite dynamic? This one is less clear, for we might imagine how seldom we would find cynics who are able to operate as a cohesive group. It's even less clear why a group would desire a fool as a figurehead. As we saw in the example of the more liberal church, it might be helpful to replace the word *cynic* with *skeptic* in this case, which is more positive. Previously, we said we often see more progressive Protestant churches who nevertheless desire a leader who seems to have a pure faith, one devoid of the skeptical uncertainty plaguing the congregation. Likewise, a group of liars in a legislature nevertheless seem to expect their leader to be a true believer. The pattern of collectives of cynics desiring a foolish leader is less clear, but deep down, we're primed to seek out someone who directly believes in a way we cannot.

The Fundamentalist Already Knows

I am arguing we must resist imagining the fundamentalist can be argued out of their faith. It is not a matter of introducing more facts, for their deepest fears already indicate their ideology is an indefensible farce, which is why they search for such obviously duplicitous counter-arguments to defend their beliefs. The religious fundamentalist postures with certainty, but the confidence is always a ruse. Žižek put it this way: "A fundamentalist does not believe, he knows it directly. Both liberal-skeptical cynics and fundamentalists share a basic underlying feature: the loss of the ability to believe, in the proper sense of the term. What is unthinkable for them is the groundless decision that installs all authentic beliefs, a decision that cannot be based on a chain of reasonings, on positive knowledge."[13] You don't have to tell fundamentalists they are wrong. They already know, for they only continue to be fundamentalists because they don't care all too much.

Peter Rollins gives an excellent example in his book *The Divine Magician.*[14] The joke begins with three figures (an Englishman, a Scotsman, and an Irishman), who are all training for a covert military operation. A sergeant entered a room with the three prospective agents and informed them they would face a final test. The violence required by the job would be troubling to the conscience, and so the higher-ups needed to be absolutely certain these recruits would be devoid of healthy emotional balance. They wanted to ensure conscience wouldn't impede the mission. As the three men sat in a waiting room, the sergeant called the Englishman first. He placed a gun on the table before the recruit and ordered him to enter the adjacent room and shoot whoever they would find inside.

The Englishman entered the room and returned only seconds later with the gun still loaded. "I'm sorry," he began, "but I'm not cut out for this. You cannot expect me to shoot my best friend."

The Scotsman was called next and given the same instructions. He entered the room, and a moment later a gunshot is heard. The recruit returned and happily reported, "I knew you couldn't ask me to actually kill my friend, and I see I was right that the gun was loaded with blanks!"

Finally the Irishman was called and sent into the room. The sergeant immediately heard the full magazine of gunshots ring, and then he heard sounds of a vicious struggle. The sergeant charged into the room to find the

13. Žižek, *How to Read Lacan*, 116.

14. Rollins, *The Divine Magician*, 158–61.

Irishman bloodied and out of breath: "Did you know someone loaded this gun with blanks?" he began. "I had to use the chair."

While we are tempted to think of the Irishman as the foolish fundamentalist, Rollins suggests the fundamentalist is actually the Scotsman: "For the Scotsman is the one who hears the manifest message (kill the guy), but who understands and obeys the implicit content of that message (don't kill the guy)."[15] Those who remain in communities requiring a high degree of dogmatic or psychotic belief can only stay insofar as they distance themselves from fully believing. To believe too much is to create the cognitive dissonance that will rupture the ideology; those who believe too strongly in a rigid system will eventually leave it. On the other hand, if someone is able to remain in a fundamentalist community well on into their adult years, it's safe to assume a significant number of disloyalties—tiny infractions against how they are supposed to behave—have been hidden. Only constant disloyalties can sustain our commitment to a system demanding absolute loyalty. There is no such thing as a fundamentalist adult who is without their massive hypocrisies, and the demand for strict loyalty is a disloyalty-producing machine.

15. Ibid., 159.

Moses and Ra

After God spoke from the burning bush, Moses turned his eyes toward the Pharaoh's palace. It was pity he felt, for the he knew what would soon come to pass under the rule of a hardened heart. He had been rescued from the Nile as an infant, and he was soon to turn the same river into blood. He demanded the Pharaoh free his slaves, but the Pharaoh laughed.

If the heart couldn't be made to understand, then the eyes would be made to see. Moses struck the river with his rod, and it became poison. Pests of every kind engulfed the lands, and the livestock fell to the ground. Boils overcame the bodies of the slaveholders, and hail poured the wrath of God upon the land. Locusts ate the crops, and darkness overcame the land when the sun was blotted out. After all of these, the Pharaoh's heart remained cold.

The final plague was visited upon the land by an angel of death. The demon swept away the firstborn of each household, and the chaos was absolute. The loss of his own son broke the Pharaoh's will, and he called Moses back into his courts. The children of Israel had won their victory through the most savage catastrophes a God had ever wrought. Moses saw himself leading the people out of the lands into another which was only promised.

From the heavens, Egypt's god Ra gazed in bemusement at Moses, who was lying deliriously on his cot in the desert heat. "What a poor soul," thought Ra, "who can do so little for his people that he must hallucinate a murderous angel to satisfy his own desire for vengeance."

7 Resentments of the Beast

The truth is happy to cast away its mask, but we wouldn't look upon it if it did. As the psychoanalyst Lacan rightly suggested, "The subject hallucinates his world,"[1] but he wasn't the first to recognize that peculiar need to believe in alternate realities. Long age, the philosopher Plato told a parable for the deaf ears of humankind.[2] In the allegory of the cave, a group of men were shackled against their will and forced to stare at the back wall of a deep cavern. The men spent their entire lives in this way, awaking every day to look at nothing but the rocky surface before them. A dim light from behind provided the only scene, as the mundanity of their lives was broken only by the occasional shadows cast across the cave's back wall.

One of the men eventually freed himself of the shackles and stumbled toward the surface. There he found the whole world, a world painful to the eyes of one who had only ever seen shadows. He saw color for the first time. He saw the trees, the fields, and the cities, and afterward he ran back into the cave to free the others. He told them of the world outside the cave, but men with no concept of a world cannot imagine the sights he describes. How would we explain color to those who had only seen shadows? He desired to bring them to the surface to see for themselves, but the men wouldn't have it. It wasn't just a case of not being able to imagine, but moreover they found their would-be liberator arrogant for supposing he knew something they couldn't yet know. Plato's allegory of the cave ends by telling us if the shackled men had been able to move, they would have killed the liberator.

1. Lacan, *On the Names-of-the-Father*, 9.
2. The allegory of the cave is in Plato, *The Republic.*

Plato may have been writing hundreds of years before the Christ and thousands of years before our time, but the execution of liberators isn't a story going out of fashion. It doesn't get old because we enjoy our repetition of whatever does not work. We've been exploring the spectrum of cynicism to foolishness, and we've begun to ask how the same symbol, creed, or ritual means so many different things to the members of the community. Morality is one of those symbols, so let us think about the genesis of morality.

Debts, Resentments, and Ressentiment

The philosopher Friedrich Nietzsche suggested we think of morality as a progression from debts to moral demands, and from moral demands to resentments, and there is a great deal we might learn from mining this genealogy of morals.[3] There was almost certainly a time when a debt was merely a financial obligation between a creditor and debtor, but at some point the relationship was no longer framed only in financial terms but also in moral terms. We accepted our duty as moral beings to repay our debts. In fact, as the social theorist David Graeber put it, the greatest tool those in power have is our belief that paying our debts is a moral issue.[4] Whether or not we agree that paying debts is a moral issue, those lending the money certainly prefer we never even consider the question.

Christianity is rife with the language of debt, and it is no accident that orthodox Christianity became associated with the proper debtor. When Saint Anselm began to formulate his theory of substitutionary atonement in the late eleventh century, his question was: why the God-man? What is the purpose of the Christ? His solution was novel, for Christianity before Anselm had felt content to leave the question mostly open. Many taught Christ was important because, in some vague sense, Christ defeated the devil and served as a ransom for humankind. Various prior figures had used language related to debt, but it was Anselm who delivered something approaching a modern formula. He argued that just as an offended lord requires the peasant to pay for the lord's wounded honor, so too a God's honor has been offended by sin. Debt in this case is not one of money, nor even of sin, but of honor. Anselm argued Christ's sacrifice must have created an imbalance such that his sacrifice for humanity canceled out the

---

3. The genealogy of morals and the later term *ressentiment* can be found in Nietzsche, *On the Genealogy of Morals.*

4. I highly recommend Graeber, *Debt.*

payment demanded by a God with wounded honor. It would be several hundred more years until Christianity began thinking of Christ in the manner common today, where Christ paid a debt not of honor but of sin. During the sixteenth-century Reformation, this framework of sin repayment became the hegemonic Protestant view. Our sin required punishment, and Christ took our deserved punishment upon himself. In a way, being a good citizen who pays one's debts became a bit Godlike.

Debt also enslaves the debtor to the lender, and a lack of power does curious things to the human psyche. Nietzsche was interested in the genesis of religion, but he wasn't content to dismiss religion as nothing but wish making and fairy tales. There must be more going on at a concrete level, and as an atheist he desired to find the concrete function. This is the story he discovered.

In the ancient Mesopotamian world, empire rose against empire while smaller tribes suffered the consequences. Even at the height of their power, the people of Israel couldn't compete against the forces of Egypt, Babylon, and Assyria. The powerful thought the opposite of *good* was *low*, and just as the opposite of the noble was the peasant, the opposite of wealthy was poverty, the opposite of clean was filth, and the opposite of power was impotence. What are those without nobility, wealth, and power to do in a situation such is this? What recourse do the powerless have? The solution was so ingenious it echoed down through the ages. Rather than accepting (1) the opposite of *good* as *low*, we would decide (2) the opposite of *good* was *evil*. The powerless rethought relationships of power as relationships of morality, and we would teach forevermore that goodness (and likewise, Godliness) are on the side of the powerless rather than the powerful. We would take the noble's idea of physical cleanliness and turn it into a sanitation of the heart. We would say the king might be in power now, but his oppression would end with the final judgment of God.

After the conversion from good versus low to good versus evil, those without power viewed their lowly position as a sign of strength. The Israelite idea spread across Europe in the mode of Christianity, which remembered its God-man savior as the most humble of servants who was killed for his perfect love. In Christianity, the Law of Moses was internalized as a demand written upon our hearts. Debt etched itself onto our hearts as well. We began to see the responsibility to pay our debts and love our neighbors as things we *must* do—because we said so and God agreed. The German Nietzsche couldn't find an appropriate word to describe this process of internalizing morality, so he used a word from French instead: *ressenti-ment*. By *ressentiment*, he meant we (1) internalize our morality and allow it to guide us, but we actually do this as a way to (2) take revenge against the powerful. Instead of the king's will to power, the weak would deploy *ressentiment* as an imaginary will to power. If Israel couldn't will itself into power and take physical revenge against its adversaries, it would instead imagine a spiritual revenge.

Ressentiment is easiest to see today among those self-righteous guardians of Truth and so-called champions of morality who demand everyone live just as they live. In recent decades, a changing world has meant slightly (and only slightly) less power for white, Christian, heterosexual, patriarchal, traditionalist, cisgender, able-bodied, American males, and they now feel oppressed. Even though they dictate nearly all of society, they feel a slightly changing world as a threatening indicator of oppression. So if they feel they cannot take physical revenge, they will imagine themselves spiritually superior. They will vote for whatever charlatan or cynic will pretend to share their values. They will duplicitously say they "love the sinner but hate the sin." They will say "all lives matter." Everything they say will be a reaction to a changing world, a world they feel they cannot physically control and must therefore imagine is beneath them.

This is *ressentiment*, an imaginary revenge making the smug guardian of Truth feel superior. He hides from his suspicions that everything he opposes is actually something he secretly desires. He condemns those who have sex because his marriage is suffering. He condemns the professors because he resents his lack of education. He condemns the Muslim because he wants to know his faith is the right one. He condemns biblical legalism even as he demands society live according to the Bible, because he desires legalism. He judges others for enjoying, because he resents the life he has not enjoyed. He condemns moral relativism, because he cannot admit his own morals are relative and flawed. He secures himself with the confidence that his views are the right ones, and so he decides anyone desiring more justice must be going *beyond* the acceptable level of justice. He is a small man who imagines himself Godlike, and every fiber of his supposedly righteous self is filled with fantasies of revenge and power. He is the man of *ressentiment*, and men such as this have a history of killing their would-be liberators.

If *ressentiment* continues to infect social dynamics, then it is a safe bet someone found it useful. The man of *ressentiment* is a fool, but the cynical leader sees him as a useful fool. The man of *ressentiment* may even be an honest fool, but he is still dangerous. The fool desires not to know, for knowledge might force him to rethink his worldview. So when the cynical charlatan sees a crowd full of vengeful *ressentiment*, he finds an opportunity to give them what their itching ears want to hear. The charlatan speaks their language of revenge by reassuring them of their righteousness. It doesn't occur to a crowd of fools how they are being taken advantage of, serving as cogs in a machine destined for pain. It never occurs that their deepest values are merely the haphazardly cobbled-together illusions and delusions exploited by the charlatan. As we said in the opening of this book, it would be a mistake to think we are subjects who desire to know; instead we are subjects who desire. Desire, especially the desire for vengeance, becomes untethered altogether in the collective.

Why the Collective (Non-)Beliefs?

The man of *ressentiment* believes a great many things in any given moment, but he will equivocate and hedge when we ask whether he truly believes in the nonsense he utters. I am claiming these easily disregarded beliefs deserve the highest scrutiny. When someone says "Well, sure, I don't necessarily believe all this," it is too often followed with "but still . . . ." We need to pay attention to the most indefensible beliefs, because those often operate even when the believer is quick to abandon them under pressure. What does it look like to have a belief kept in place for some functional value even when nobody directly believes? Can a belief still do something when nobody defends it? My wager is, yes, beliefs continue to operate regardless of whether they appear important to the ideologue, and there's no better example of collective beliefs that function—regardless of whether anyone actually, directly believes in them—than the conspiracy theory. From the Latin word meaning to breathe together (*conspirare*), a conspiracy theory grabs the culture's attention by suggesting something important was missed by the official narrative. Though I admit being highly skeptical of conspiracy theories and don't believe in any of those I'll survey below, understanding how they work delivers a crucial insight to how beliefs operate even when nobody directly, unequivocally believes them (such as with the religious or political fundamentalist). I'm arguing that a conspiracy theory provides an example for how the dynamics of collective belief work, even when the belief is so ridiculous it's immediately disavowed or left unacknowledged.

It's difficult to know from the start which idea is merely a ludicrous conspiracy theory because, of course, occasionally the most audacious explanation turns out to be true. For example, when news broke of the Watergate scandal, one could be forgiven for doubting President Nixon's involvement. Before it became clear Iraq had no weapons of mass destruction, how many would have believed a reporter claiming the evidence was fabricated? So instead of thinking of conspiracies as merely outlandish claims, we need to think about (1) what makes a belief specifically unwarranted and (2) why it's being propagated in the first place. What are the features of false collective beliefs, and why do they have staying power?

We find a number of fairly consistent traits with unwarranted conspiratorial beliefs.[5] (1) They always *claim the official narrative is false*. The media presents some initial story, and just as quickly there arises an alternative version claiming the media's story must be false simply because it is the official story. (2) The conspiracy theorist always *assumes the real intentions are nefarious*. Nobody ever seems to plot a secret plan in order to do mass good, and instead, the cabal is always a group of powerful people with the means, motive, and opportunity to cause destruction. (3) Conspiracies depend on tying together the catastrophic problem with some other seemingly *unrelated events*. After a big event, the official story will say Actor A did Something B leading to Event C. But the conspiracy theorist notices another Something X also happened at the same time. It is this seemingly unrelated event X that provides the meat for the theory. This also means evidence for the conspiracy theory is usually circumstantial, not direct. (4) Though the conspiring actors are often very public figures, the actors are always presumed able to keep their plans a *well-guarded secret*. Whether the actors are unknown agents or politicians, a conspiracy always assumes they were able to keep the plans out of public light until a rogue reporter decided to dig deeper. Finally, (5) the chief tool of any conspiracy is *errant data*, which might simply be more data left unaccounted for in the official narrative, or it may actually be data that blatantly contradicts the facts as we know them. As a tool to support outlandish beliefs, contradictory data is most interesting to us because it boldly acknowledges from the beginning how unlikely the belief will be. Because of boldness (since we tend to assume someone wouldn't say something so outlandish without reason), our natural tendency is to feel intrigued.

5. These characteristics of conspiracy theories are adapted from Keeley, "Of Conspiracy Theories."

None of these factors together mean the conspiratorial belief is automatically wrong, but the factors do suggest a problematic structure. Nevertheless, our society gravitates toward conspiracy theories. Most are merely interesting without being too consequential. In other words, even if it were true we faked the moon landing or if JFK was assassinated by the CIA, it wouldn't affect NASA today or suggest a president will be assassinated again. If a conspiracy turned out to be true, it would change our historical narrative but usually not our present circumstance. On the other hand, there are conspiracy theories that are credulous and unmerited while also directly affecting the world in which we live. Even if nobody admits belief in them, they can be believed indirectly as a collective. I wager conspiratorial thinking is indeed occasionally stoked with great precision, and this is done to control the religiopolitical tribe.

If I brush aside something you consider important, you'll have to forgive my skepticism. My only interest is in how conspiracy theories uncover something about collective (non-)belief, especially for what they suggest about faith. So let's quickly consider the conspiracies around 9/11, which claim it was not a result of foreign terrorism but instead an inside job for nefarious purposes. Whether we judge those conspiracies true or false, we might notice those who believe 9/11 was an inside job demonstrate each of the five features we listed above. First, the official narrative must be false because it was the easiest narrative to reach. The attack fit right perfectly with the desire to launch a war for control of oil, it hid financial records, or it just couldn't be the case that nineteen hijackers could coordinate such wanton destruction. At any rate, the conspiratorial thinker decides the official narrative cannot be trusted. It's not much of a leap to then assume, secondly, the real intentions were much more nefarious. Third, the conspiracy thinker emphasizes the collapse of the World Trade Center building 7 (in addition to the two towers struck) and sees it as evidence of something else. Or they claim footage from nearby security cameras near the Pentagon was collected and never released. They ask of the relations between the Bush family and the Bin Laden family. They ask why a plane struck the Pentagon at the exact point where remodeling ensured minimal casualties. As for errant data, were cell phones in 2001 were capable of making calls from 30,000 feet? These are all common points from the 9/11 "truther" movement, questions attempting to construct a counter-narrative based on events which, at first sight, do not seem to have anywhere to fit within the official account. The questions are loaded, and though some are better than others, each relies on the hearer to make a connection between a piece of errant data and the conclusion that the conspiracy theorist desires.

Let's consider an older theory to test this schema further. When the Oklahoma City bombing first hit the news, the culprit, Timothy McVeigh, was captured rather quickly. But rather than being captured because of a massive manhunt, he was pulled over when a traffic cop simply noticed his vehicle had no license plate. The officer asked if McVeigh was armed, at which point McVeigh politely informed the officer, yes, he was armed but did not have the license for the gun. He was taken to jail and held for the offense, and while he was being held his name was released as the main suspect. "How convenient," says the conspiracy believer, "that a man with such supposed know-how would make such an elementary mistake ensuring a quick capture." The conspiracy believer rejects the official narrative and then notices that while the Bureau of Alcohol, Tobacco, and Firearms maintained an office in the building bombed, not one agent was in the building at the time of the attack. A separate conspiracy theory emerged to claim the ATF was conducting a sting operation—perhaps even supplying McVeigh with the bomb and opportunity as a set-up—and then lost track of him shortly before the bombing (with only enough time to warn their people out of harm's way).

Anniversaries are a common tool for conspiracy theories as a way to tie together events which are seemingly unrelated. Those who considered McVeigh guilty pointed to his being upset at the federal raid on the Branch Davidian compound in Waco, Texas only two years before the day of the bombing. But those who doubted McVeigh's guilt suspected the true culprit of the Oklahoma City bombing was the Japanese government. The Oklahoma City bombing happened one month after a sarin gas attack on a Tokyo subway, and a separate theory pinned the blame for the sarin gas attack on the CIA. So if we are the type of person who believes in the ties between seemingly unrelated events, it is not a huge leap to think that Oklahoma might have been international payback for Tokyo.

These examples mix various facts and erroneous data, but none of them seem to be practically useful. If the only reason I engage conspiratorial thought in this book is to examine the usefulness of collective beliefs, let's turn to a more recent example alive in American politics today. There is a persistent belief claiming Barak Obama is not a natural-born citizen of the United States, which pairs with suspicions that an untold number of actors worked in collusion to keep Obama's real citizenship secret. Believers in this conspiracy theory are often called "birthers." Though we may only very rarely encounter people in real life who overtly claim Obama is not a citizen, all of our statistical evidence suggests the this conspiratorial belief is rampant. As many as three in four Republicans are at least open to the idea (as well as a not-insignificant number of Democrats and independents).[6] The birther conspiracy shows us more than simply how a conspiracy begins. It shows us why.

I have yet to meet a person who claims to believe in the birther conspiracies, but surveys suggest I interact with birthers every single day. Consider the irony here, especially as we think about how people (halfway) believe something they do not act as if they believe. After all, it makes little sense for Democrats and independents to vote for someone they halfway consider Constitutionally ineligible. On the other side, only around one in three Republicans say they are certain Obama is not a citizen. If we include those who think it's at least possible he is not a citizen, we arrive at roughly three-quarters of all Republican-leaning voters. At no point has any survey shown even half of Republicans certain Obama is eligible to be President as a natural-born citizen. Few openly admit belief in this conspiracy theory, but doesn't a disavowed belief still sway votes?

After the release of his long-form birth certificate in 2011, belief in Obama's citizenship rose quickly. But it's also interesting to consider this happened just days before he announced the killing of Osama Bin Laden, which naturally boosted his public approval and likely would have boosted belief in his citizenship as well. After all, people don't respond to surveys based on facts alone. We saw an example of this when we discussed how around one in four people will tell a pollster the sun revolves around the earth. There are limits to polls, but they suggest something about how we simply desire, rather than desire to know. There are a lot of reasons we say we believe as we do, and it's not always because we actually believe them. The number of people believing in Obama's citizenship dropped again before the 2012 election, and pundits noticed not one of his potential opponents in the Republican primary field would clearly admit Obama was a citizen. This is not because the primary contenders were wrong on the facts—they were all perfectly capable and educated individuals—but they would have been seen as an outsider if they rejected what so many within their party believe (or at least, what many say or think they believe). They knew they were expected to lie, because the birther conspiracy had become

6. Berinsky, "The Birthers Aren't Going Anywhere (An Update)."

a floating signifier for Republican. One shouldn't blaspheme the holy spirit by spitting upon the creed.

We reap what we sow. If we cultivate a lie as part of our personal history, we must eventually either admit the lie or repress it further with more lies. When a party cultivates a delusional belief as a key signifier, it either risks the heresy of truth-telling or keeps up the ruse with increasing bravado. In fact, the winner of the 2016 presidential election selected the birther conspiracy theory as his point of entry into populist politics, knowing it would create a sense of trust he could use to mobilize a campaign years later. If there is one thing the cynic has, it is both arrogance and deep self-doubt masquerading as bravado.

There are far more examples, and extremist views so often depend on conspiracy theories to create a useful interpretation filter. Consider the belief that anthropocentric climate change is nothing but a hoax. This belief implicates practically all climate scientists as a secret cabal scheming for some supposed anti-business agenda, but the actual purpose of supporting such conspiratorial thinking is, obviously, the deregulation of energy production, which in turn yields higher profits for non-renewable energy companies. If a ridiculous conspiracy theory is being supported by media and the establishment, it is because it works in someone's interests. If a conspiracy theory is useful, it becomes encoded into an ideological program just as a virus infects software. Just as this book is not about conspiracies but about the different ways ideas are deployed, our interest here is not really with politics or even simply with theology. Our interest throughout this book is how all belief functions, collectively and individually. As we have seen, it seems belief always includes a false consciousness, which is a perception conditioned by class and other environmental factors beyond our awareness or control. Some amount of fiction is healthy. When a child says she feels she is the smartest or fastest or kindest in her class, only a parent with deeply seated insecurities would correct the child. The problem comes when a relationship between two people is also a relationship between different languages and motives, when one's false consciousness doesn't match the other's, and when we risk without the possibility of reward. Once false consciousness is encoded, it will prove difficult to debug.

Encoding Our False Consciousness

Repetition works hand-in-hand with the desire not to know. Repetition of behaviors within a given class of society creates a false consciousness which appears normative; the values and judgments issuing forth from that class-based false consciousness are soon called "common sense." Repetition encodes the habit until the habit becomes second nature. Sometimes even the desire not to repeat a past mistake acts to ensure we do repeat, which is borne out every time we say "This idea didn't work before, so let us try harder again." Our knowledge becomes selective, and we seek out sources of information justifying views we already hold. We might have access to all the information ever gathered with only a moment's glance at our smartphones, but we haven't let go of our gullibility. We believe more than ever, and whereas we once believed in our priests and leaders, and we know believe in our social media streams. We once believed in our flags and traditions, and we have abandoned them for the schizophrenia of whatever cause of the week presents itself. This is not entirely a bad thing, but what is the end goal of this frantic activity of identity crafting?

Perhaps the goal of frantic identity crafting in a social media age can be likened to a collective schizophrenia. In their book *Anti-Oedipus*, the philosophers Gilles Deleuze and Félix Guattari proposed that previously important identities continually break down, and new identities are perpetually encoded. This encoding works in much the same way as a computer program. Once a flaw is discovered in a program, an update is rushed to keep users engaged. If we lost the church as the hub of social connection, we logged onto Facebook instead. If we no longer tithe, we donate instead to GoFundMe or Amnesty International. If we no longer have confession, we opt for therapy. If we lose the assurance of divine approval, we need new ways to prop up our narcissism. Narcissism itself was reinvented, and we now view those who aren't constantly posting about their lives on social media as being antisocial. To be social is now to be narcissistic, and we take it as a virtue rather than vice. Narcissism is unstable and needs to reassure itself, so it continually encodes itself in new ways.

In a very literal way, encoding debts gave rise to religion. Archaeologists tell us ancient Mesopotamian temples acted almost like a bank before there were coins in circulation.[7] There is a pervasive myth that economy (1)

---

7. For a fascinating history of debt and an exploration of the relationship between credit and ancient temples, I again recommend Graeber, *Debt*.

began with bartering, and then we eventually (2) invented coins, and finally we became sophisticated enough to tally up (3) credit. This is an old myth, but newer archaeological evidence suggests the process was almost the exact opposite. We invented credit, then coins, and only occasionally did we barter if and when currency went out of circulation. In brief, our ancestors would have worked a day in the temple and receive a credit, which would be tallied up on a clay tablet. Perhaps the credit tally would be equal to tens bushels of wheat or one goat (the unit of exchange doesn't matter for our purposes), and then our ancestor could give one of her credits to a neighbor in exchange for work done. In this society, to not participate in temple worship was much more serious than simply being a religious heretic; to not worship in the temple meant our ancestor would be cut off from the village's primitive economy. Survival actually depended on our work being encoded upon the clay tablets sitting next to the stone gods.

We use digital bank records instead of clay tablets today, but our desires are encoded just the same. If we want to see what you desire, we needn't ask what conspiratorial beliefs or social causes you stand firmly behind; we need only look at how your desires have been encoded in your bank statements. Desire eats, it breathes, and it heats. It is our lusts, fantasies, and needs, but it was a mistake to ever think it was a single thing. No matter how much we'd like to think of ourselves as rational beings, we are desiring machines. Encoding simply made us readable, even if we can't quite read ourselves.

Except sometimes encoding doesn't work out the way society expects, and certain conditions of mental illness show us not only (1) how antisocial behaviors stand out but also (2) how society actively creates the very illnesses against which it defines itself. Not only should we destigmatize illness, but we should also recognize we all suffer a range of symptoms; if we are not labeled, it is because our peculiarities are not (yet) regulated by hegemony. Psychosis is a perfect example of how theology works today, where a religious group actively encodes certain behaviors and beliefs that would be considered odd under different circumstances. If someone speaks to an imaginary partner, she isn't trying to flaunt social norms. She simply doesn't experience certain social commands (against talking to oneself or disrupting public space). In cases of psychosis, the patient does not experience the big Other's injunction against certain behaviors. Or put another way, if my big Other commands X and your big Other commands Y, our behaviors will appear antisocial to each other but not to ourselves. Like the story of the girl who lost her parents and nevertheless continued trying to please them, it wouldn't do much good to tap the shoulder of someone talking to an imaginary friend and ask if they realize nobody is there—of course they can see nobody is there, but they hear the accusations all the same. Those accusations from the big Other—the memory of whomever we are trying to please regardless of whether the big Other even exists—demand a response. We all have moments of psychosis inside us. Psychoanalysis is over once the patient realizes the big Other does not exist.

Let us step backward to this claim that we are all a kind of schizophrenic today, all captured in the snares of a capitalist society that perpetually demands we create new versions of ourselves. We are told to accumulate, to strive, and to encode our new identities, so one finds a hobby while another finds religion. Deleuze and Guattari said we must need a new kind of psychoanalysis, a schizoanalysis, an analysis for a psychotic society whose identity is always in flux. And as odd as all this sounds, there was actually some concrete use of this theory in a space where we'd least expect.

Jonah Peretti, the founder and CEO of the popular website Buzzfeed, was shaped by his research on Deleuze and Guattari's schizoanalysis. In an essay discussing this philosophical vantage point, he wrote, "Identity formation is inextricably linked to the urge to consume, and therefore the acceleration of capitalism necessitates an increase in the rate at which individuals assume and shed identities. The internet is one of many late capitalist phenomena allowing more flexible, rapid, and profitable mechanisms of identity formation."[8] Thusly so he described how we inscribe new identities in spaces online. His website's article and video content is built around the idea of viral sharing on social media. If our world is always creating and abolishing identities at every moment, and if people seem to desire new identities and causes like one gasping for air, then why not make a business of it? Buzzfeed is successful because it is viral. It is viral because its flashy headlines and quick content make us look cultured, clever, or relaxed when we share it to Twitter and Facebook, and since we are narcissists with a need to be seen, we shared Peretti's website and made him a millionaire. All we do is for the encoding of the economy. All we do is for the gaze of the big Other. After all, the big Other is a cruel task-master demanding we pretend to enjoy, live life to the fullest, be informed, be righteous, or whatever else. Demands can't stop, because just as the old gods had to be worshiped in temples for the primitive exchange of wheat and goats, the

---

8. Peretti, "Capitalism and Schizophrenia."

new gods demand we encode ourselves with an online brand. If the new gods didn't succeed in gathering our participation, our economy would stop its motion.

This is how unconscious repetition works, for it encodes a brutal big Other. We call the big Other our friends, jobs, causes, gods, or whatever else. Viral videos, important causes, and witty memes create an identity that will last for an ephemeral moment and then disappear to make room for the next. We are told to promote certain ideas and feel rage toward others, but we are always told to encode ourselves moment to moment. But every so often an idea becomes more than an empty meme. Sometimes it becomes catastrophic.

The demand for new housing investments led Wall Street to create the subprime mortgage market, which encoded an identity (homeowner, middle class) until it became too expansive and crashed in 2008. Encoding works until it does not. The big Other works until it does not. The versions of ourselves we project work until they do not. Our habits work until they become addictions. Ideologies work until they require conspiracies to prop up their emptiness. Desire is continuously stoked, because someone's paycheck depends on continuous encoding. The cynical charlatan does not care about your important social causes; he only hopes we care enough to keep our frantic activity in motion. Faith depends on unconscious pleasure, and so we hold on to our beliefs exactly as strongly as the pleasure they yield. So when does one paradigm get dropped and another adopted, and what does this tell us about the way religion operates? What does it take for the faulty encoding to undergo a cascading collapse, a chain reaction that requires a new program?

Ideology Is a Paradigm

Let me extend the software metaphor for encoding just a bit further. We've likely all continued using glitchy software applications even though an update is available to resolve the glitch. If you are like me, you might wait a year before finally updating your laptop to resolve the issue, but once it's done, it's done. One doesn't revert backward, only forward, and the software update happens in an instant that changes the encoding of my laptop forever. When I don't update, it's because it's either inconvenient to fix a problem or because I fear I'll lose information in the process. I continue using something that doesn't work well because it is easier to maintain my routines. Our religious, political, and cultural ideological paradigms are re-encoded in much the same fashion.

The various identities with which we are encoded feel precious and must be guarded. We might like to pretend our various identity markers (the products we consume, teams for which we cheer, gods we worship) are not so important, but the very fact that we invest any energy at all in defending our identity markers (especially the doctrinal) already suggests we are invested more than we suspect. Likewise, it's when someone tells you she doesn't care at all that you know you've hit a nerve. It isn't unusual for one to say "I was betrayed, but I'm over it" or for another to say "I was raised that way, but I've moved on." If we probe further into their history and quickly see further rebuttals, we intuitively know the person is hiding anxiety from herself. In the face of composed indifference we see internal conflict. Ideas are guarded with a great many stories having nothing to do with the idea being defended. Again, the classic question of analysis: which is the symptom, and which is the cause? Is this flaw a feature or a bug?

Just as important is another question: when should we start to think of symptom overload as evidence we judged wrongly about the cause? When do we stop saying "We need better arguments" and instead decide all the problems in our ideology are actually caused by something encoded deeply within the underlying paradigm? Theology and science have very different ways of dealing with this problem, so maybe we have something to learn from the scientists.

The philosopher of science Thomas Kuhn struck into controversial fame when he suggested scientific progress isn't always a matter of slowly building atop older theories with new evidence.[9] Occasionally discoveries force us to reorient our entire approach, and he called this a paradigm shift. For example, when Copernicus discovered the heliocentric model and Galileo confirmed it with his telescope, the new model wasn't immediately more predictively reliable than the geocentric model. To leap from one model to the other was not simply a matter of deciding which produced more accurate observations. Examples abound throughout our science textbooks—a challenge to the corpuscular theory, an observation of the changing heavens when a star turns into a supernova, the advance of medical science once we abandoned humors and leeches, the realization that Newtonian physics failed to account for Einstein's relativity—suggesting there are two kinds of science. (1) There is normal science taught in text-

9. See Kuhn, *The Structure of Scientific Revolutions.*

books, in which new ideas build atop old ideas as new evidence mounts. (2) There is also a paradigm-shifting science leaping from one entire model to another. A shift from one theory to the newer model is sometimes as arbitrary as the older generation simply dying off and leaving new generation of professors teaching newer ideas.

If you've had a serious, paradigm-shifting change of mind during your life, did it happen slowly or in an instant? It can happen either way, but while we like to imagine we construct our knowledge with acute precision and reason, a paradigm often shifts in a flash. In an instant, we know our worldview has changed. We didn't ask for it, didn't expect it, and can't blame ourselves for never seeing it coming. We will defend the most indefensible ideas with creative justifications, and entire fields of apologetics hide themselves in the bowels of libraries and the hyperlinks of blogs that rarely feel the gaze of the anxious believer until anxiety is triggered. We are anxious that we might be wrong, so we seek out justification to keep the paradigm shift on hold. Anxiety triggers doubts further and further, and the beast of poor ideas feeds its fill.

If we are hunched over old books and reading apologetic defenses for our views, it is because we already know, deep down where we cannot bear to explore, that our views are indeed indefensible. When talking to a defensive person, a direct test of strength won't be an effective way to dismantle the absurd idea. The entrenched belief is only routed indirectly, from the flanks, and ultimately it is uprooted because the believer no longer desires the idea. Again, if your beliefs have changed rather significantly at least once in your life, you know exactly how this pattern feels. The paradigm was killed by song, a work of art, an unexpected quip from a friend, or perhaps a book. You didn't know this singularly important paradigm was about to leave you forever.

Beliefs are chipped away—bits and pieces here and there begin to fall apart—but the cluster of ideology remains for the most part unchanged until a very specific idea loses significance. You find out something didn't happen the way you thought, and your paradigm collapses.

Belief is a network, and one seemingly innocuous (but severely problematic) idea can hide among others. If we found the cause of the idea, we might resolve the symptoms; but its rare to really find the cause. In fact, we enjoy our symptoms, because continuing with what doesn't work is more pleasurable than the hard work of change. The cause of a symptom is also inside a network, and networks lie without end.

To illustrate how we kill off problematic viewpoints (symptoms) in order to keep intact a problematic paradigm (cause), let's consider the most obvious example of a network. If we were to map out hyperlinks between all sites on the Internet, it would be extremely clear which sites were the big companies and which sites were not. If one cluster connects to billions of others, it is Google or Facebook and nothing else. Suppose we desired to remove one website but hoped to keep the Internet basically unchanged. It would be clear which sites we probably shouldn't delete. The body desires homeostasis; the mind desires epistemic stasis. Given the choice between anxiety and change on the one hand or entrenching to keep the world stable, you know what we tend to do.

All networks desire stability. Removing the big, clustered connections would do irreparable harm to the Internet, so given the choice we would opt to delete an unknown and unconnected site rather than the bulk. It is the same with ideas, but there comes a caveat: it is often the most indefensible point which supports the big cluster. The big cluster of beliefs we adopted to tell us who we are, why we are here, and whether our lives have meaning—this cluster must be protected at all costs. It is like a scientific theory guarded by a bulk of data, and the destruction of one small piece of data does not cause the bulk of the theory to collapse. Except sometimes it does.

Religion does something oddly different with paradigms, and we might meditate on whether we are so different from the priests who protested Copernicus and Galileo based on a literal reading of a very geocentric Bible. Consider how chaotic it would be if we discovered one small part of our worldview actually supported all the rest. Haven't we seen those who defend the most indefensible belief not because they actually desire to believe it but instead because it is a logical extension of something else they wish to believe? Have we the prescience to notice this problem in ourselves? There are the Big Cluster Ideas, and there are the small, secondary or tertiary ideas that developed to support it.

For example, if I suggest the theory of evolution is true and someone feels anger, I know (1) they are feeling anxiety, and (2) anxiety has nothing to do with evolution or creationism. What they are feeling instead is the need to defend a secondary idea. If they lose their belief in creationism, then they fear Genesis is dubious. If Genesis is unreliable, then they fear the same about the rest of their Scripture, which casts doubt on God, which casts doubt on everything from an afterlife to their meaning in this life.

When we defend a seemingly unimportant idea—which has nothing to do with our day-to-day existence—it is because the secondary idea is guarding another. Put differently, we misrecognize our anxiety as confidence. We do this not because we are fools but because we are humans. Just as it would be deeply troubling to discover all of Google's connections were actually relying on one small server on the verge of overload, the realization that so much of our Big Cluster Ideas are supported by the smallest, most irrelevant points is indeed troubling.

On the occasion when an entire scientific paradigm is found to actually rely on one piece of faulty data, the paradigm itself falls into question. The critics set their eyes upon the downfall of the dominant paradigm and raise their glasses to toast its demise. This occasionally happens, but more commonly the big scientific paradigm changes because the old regime dies off and a new cadre, trained in the newest idea, takes its seat at the table. It is not so very different with religions, politics, and cultures.

It's rare for the establishment theologians to admit their life's project was wrong. It's rare for politicians to admit a vote was in error. It's rare for an adult with childish ideology to mature. Even when everyone starts to realize there was a fatal flaw all along for a losing cause, the soldiers stay in their trench down to the last man. When we hear, "We must defend [Cause X] or else lose our purpose altogether!" we are hearing the final breaths of an orthodoxy whose anxieties are showing. Why defend the indefensible?—because the indefensible became our whole world. The indefensible belief is filled with *ressentiment* and guards against anxiety. But it is a symptom to which we cling because we enjoy the lost object. We are nostalgic for a perfect society that never existed, and we aim to believe in the absolutes we shall never discover. So those who prefer to sleep will carry on and defend their orthodoxies. Of course, orthodoxy is simply what we desperately cling to because we had nothing much to say about the doctrine itself.

Diogenes and Alexander

Diogenes the Cynic was once sunning himself on the city streets when Alexander the Great entered Athens. When the Master enters, the whole world waits for orders. Nearly two millennia later, Martin Luther would rightly observe that every peasant desires to be a lord, a lord a noble, a noble a prince, a prince a king, and a king a god. The same desire infects the philosophers of every age, and so many of the philosophers end up serving the Master. Men of learning and their disciples who hope to become sages alike wait upon the word of the Master.

Alexander, a student of Aristotle himself and no stranger to the antics and oddities of philosophers, took a liking to Diogenes for reasons about which we can only speculate. Perhaps he believed Diogenes had eyes to see and ears to hear. Perhaps he found Diogenes sharper than any of his advisors. Perhaps he simply had the feeling so many of us do when encountering a person who has such unflinching confidence to speak the truth in a world of flattering lies.

No Master goes a day without hearing flattering and lies, and the Master would have us imagine he knows this and laments the trouble it causes. He would have us believe he is an honest man, and he would prefer we imagine it is only his important duties and unending requirements causing him to do the brutal things he does. The Master would have us believe he is a pragmatist who stalls on what needs to be done for the sake of expediency. He says things like, "Let us not forsake the better in the pursuit of the best," but he seems to accomplish neither. The world bows to the Master's logic, which makes those who do not bow a peculiar case for attention.

While walking the streets, Alexander the Great gazed upon the poor and homeless heretic lying on the ground as he bathed in the sun. The famed crazy man of Athens captured Alexander's respect as one who possessed neither the wherewithal nor the desire to impress emperors. Here was a man too direct to tell lies.

Alexander asked the dog, "My friend Diogenes! Tell me, is there anything I could do for you today? Name your desire, and it will be yours." With hubris of a man who feels no respect for position, Diogenes replied: "Could you stand out of the sun?"

8 Orthodoxy's Anxiety

If orthodoxy is that to which we desperately cling when we really haven't anything to contribute about the doctrine itself, then we must consider the role of the cynical charlatan posturing as orthodox. It's nothing unique to religion, for every field has its orthodoxies and leaders, both the honest and the deceptive. Try questioning the importance of capitalism in an economics department, Shakespeare in literature, or Euclid in mathematics, and you will discover every field has its orthodoxies. Orthodoxies are standard narratives, and they are important for cohesion. Questions produce anxiety, which leads to doubt, so orthodoxy guards against anxiety by ensuring the heretical question never arises in the first place. Sealing off space from questions posed by the heretic is a dangerous practice. When the heretics inevitably arise, the leader must choose between engaging the question or expelling the questioner. The charlatan is the cynical leader who adopts the party line and will never deviate; he's no fool.

The Charlatan

There is a fascinating documentary called *Marjoe* (1972), a film following a comeback tour of the evangelist Marjoe Gortner. From the age of four, Marjoe's parents had paraded him around the American Pentecostal South through tent revivals, television shows, and churches. They portrayed their son as a uniquely gifted child preacher. His name is quite literally a contraction of Mary and Joseph, awkwardly indicating his production as a cultural icon was in the works long before he had any choice in the matter. He was ostensibly God's gift to a world in need of revival, but really he was groomed by calculating parents who foresaw the cash they could yield through their young actor. And he was an actor. At the beginning of the documentary, he tells the camera he cannot remember a time when he ever believed in God.

Revivalist Christianity has always had a problem with con men. In nineteenth-century America, revival preachers told their listeners to never trust a theologian educated in seminary. Trust yourself, they said, and assume your reading of Scripture is as good as those who read Greek. After the Azusa Street Revival in Los Angeles during the first decade of the twentieth century, the growing Pentecostal movement produced a lot of good, and yet its emphasis on an untameable Holy Spirit meant God might well be speaking through anyone. All one needed was the confidence to proclaim God's voice and a community willing to believe. The ability to self-proclaim divine authority along with the crowd's desire for miracles made the Pentecostal movement ripe for those con men who would take advantage. The *Marjoe* documentary features lower-middle–class, rural Americans who are clearly coming to the tent for a night of escape from the mundanity of their existence. The revival is the site of intrigue and mystery, meaning and hope. It is the event where the Spirit speaks in tongues through the young and old alike, where miraculous healing is normal, where people fall to the ground and convulse with divine euphoria, and where truth is imparted by those speaking with the full force of God. The revival is also where unending flows of cash purchases the continuation of the revival cycle.

Marjoe tells a tragic story of escaping the world of fundamentalist religion only to return as his money dries up. He tells the camera of how an older preacher once pulled him aside and explained how to get rich in this business. "If I say on the radio 'I know one person out there has ten dollars saved in a jar—the Lord wants you to send the money in faith,'" the older preacher explained, "then there will be a hundred elderly women who send me their last ten dollars. It's that easy." Marjoe found the revival business immensely lucrative, but it wore on his soul. He left the faith in his teen years and found a lover, he experienced the world and traveled his fill, and he returned to the revival circuit once his funding was exhausted just as a dog returns to its vomit.

He sits with the camera crew and explains what will happen when they film his comeback revival tour. Marjoe tells the crew when they should focus in on particular churchgoers: when someone starts shivering or muttering, they are about to fall down and convulse—make sure you get it on camera. Girls will talk to you, he tells them, but follow my lead and only bring girls back to your hotel rooms if you met them outside the event—we don't want to be caught. If the revivalists ask you whether you are saved, show no equivocation whatsoever—answer with an emphatic "Yes, yes, my brother, I am washed in the Spirit!" No smoking, of course, and don't give the crowds any reason to try to convert you. Keep the ruse going.

In one of the more revealing interviews, Marjoe is asked if he considers himself a con man. Not quite, he tells us, because he's giving people the experience they want. This is what he is paid to do. In fact, if he had to pick a religion, he says he would likely choose Pentecostalism for its energy and camaraderie. Aside from the big farce of his business, he asks, what is there to despise?

If you were converted at his revivals and later saw him admitting everything, how would you feel? In the ancient church, a similar question arose over whether sacraments were still valid once the unrighteous priest was found to be a cynic merely posing as pious. The Church establishment learned of these impostor priests because the people protested. Rather than call the entire system into question and leave the Church, the masses accepted a work-around, an *ad hoc* argument to keep things just different enough so things remained basically the same. If the question was whether the sacrament was still valid even when the priest was corrupt, the church worked out a solution. The sacrament was valid so long as the priest was ordained by the Church. It's the big chain of spiritual authority which confers holiness, not the individual actions of the hypocrite and the charlatan. This awkward argument was the Church's solution to corruption. Of course, this rule is only necessary when you already assume your clergy are corrupt.

To those rural community members who gathered at each of Marjoe's revivals, the event was more real than their everyday lives. According to ticket sales, the Academy Award-winning documentary was not well-received when it released in 1972. In fact, it was so controversial many cinemas declined to show it at all. I wonder what it would've felt like to be one of those people who spoke in tongues and convulsed on the ground after being blessed by someone now admitting to being a con man on the screen. What would they think of their speaking in tongues or miraculous healings if they saw their revival preacher admit it was all a mind trick? What does it ever mean when we find an important event in our lives was contrived, when the most life-altering event was merely a farce?

The Prodigal's Name

Orthodoxy feels safe because it doesn't move. Orthodoxy sits right where we left it, verified by the authorities and trustworthy enough to ward off our anxieties. Of course, if the desire for orthodoxy and control is linked to anxiety (which always creates doubts), then orthodoxy is the very cause of questioning orthodoxy. There is a parable you already know of mercy and anxiety. In the Gospel of Luke, chapter fifteen, the teacher told of a man with two sons. Only the older son was dependable, which is to say servile. The other set eyes set on becoming a prodigal. No, that's not quite it—nobody ever intends to destroy themselves, but the unconscious tendencies for repetition and sabotage are there underneath all our ambition. The father owned land, and the ambitious son did not want to own the land. He demanded from his father an early inheritance. The laws of economy always tells us whose belongings we should own. The younger son then set off for a distant country.

He squandered his money in short order. We know not on what, but upon what does any young man squander money? He spread his wings only to collapse underneath the weight of his desire. He imagined his father accepting him back, and the fantasy became reality. The father was loving, and he welcomed the son back home. He did this in spite of the vehement protests of the servile son, the prodigal's older brother who was loyal, who kept his duty, and who couldn't formulate his own desire. The father told the older son what he should desire, namely, he should desire to stay loyal so every last penny of the father's wealth eventually pass to the son who never strayed. In the Gospel's telling, the older son is content with the father's answer. The answer was satisfying, for if all the remaining wealth passed to the older son, he would rule his penniless brother the same way his father had ruled him.

We call the father merciful and the young, ambitious son a sinner saved by immeasurable grace. The son will be forever in debt to his father, and we have an awkward habit of linking debt to freedom. The most common example is the credit card, for we are allowed luxuries on the condition we will forever be indebted to one bank or another. What if the greatest sin in the parable was not the prodigal son's flight and loose living but instead the father's monstrous enslavement of his son in the language of grace?

This question is not my own. Kester Brewin noticed the parable of the Prodigal can be read as any number of coming-of-age tales until it gets to the end, for in Brewin's alternate reading the conclusion seems a tragedy.[1] Maturity needs an awful lot of immaturity to come before it, and we learn through our mistakes in a world that teaches through consequences. We are harmed and we harm, we suffer and we squander, and we fear and we strive. We shed versions of ourselves in the process, and no matter how much the process of growth hurts, very few would wish to trade our experiences for an entirely different course. For better or worse, our experience shape us irrevocably and become a part of us. To lose our experiences would be to lose ourselves. In Brewin's reading, losing oneself is precisely happened in this parable of the Prodigal Son.

Every year a new cohort of students goes off to college. Some are the responsible son, others the rebellious. Some discover new ways of seeing the world, new ideas, experiences, and cultures. Other students will lament years later that they did not discover these things in their formative years. Some sons and daughters clash with parents and are accepted, some clash with parents and distance results. Some never clash. Some clash for a while and, after the four years pass, they betray their new experiences and revert to an older way of life in order to make their parents or their culture proud.

If the parable of the Prodigal is a coming-of-age tale, the father is the parent whose command is so unquestioned that to return home is to give in to the demands of a previous epoch. It's like the college student who visits home but pretends the to be the same person she was back in high school. The ambitious, rebellious son gave up his travels for the safety of a lifelong dependence to a father who saw nothing wrong with the arrangement. If the Christ meant this parable to be an analogue for the love of a God, it is a peculiar tale about the nature of security, orthodoxy, and anxiety.

While thinking about the role family identity takes in creating the individual, Lacan calls this idea of submission the *Name-of-the-Father*.[2] The father gives us his name, but we are expected to take much more than the family surname alone. There are also moral standards, family histories, cultural traditions, and unquestionable responsibilities. We enter a family as an infant, a bundle of pure instinct, but we are shaped into the latest image of a Name-of-the-Father. If the Name is a hateful one, be on your guard, for you will be assailed with temper and addiction. If the Name is a gracious one, the control (and damage) will be much more difficult to detect.

---

1. I highly recommend Brewin, *Mutiny!*
2. See the development of this idea in Lacan, *On the Names-of-the-Father.*

The Christ had a Name-of-the-Father separating the divine drive in the world from the ritual structures built up around this drive. Embracing a divine drive meant he intentionally squandered his reputation among sinners, he rebelled against his authorities at every encounter, and he never considered re-entering the fold of Nazarene carpenters from which he came. If he wanted to teach grace, the parable works simply enough. But what an odd story with a double edge, because it's less clear why an itinerant, rebel storyteller would tell a story which could be abused to praise the betrayal of our experiences for the safety of the well-known home.

Job's Betrayal and Three Excuses for Calamity

There is another story worth considering if we are thinking about how this primal Name-of-the-Father, along with its associated baggage, comes to shape us and become our own name. It's another always misunderstood story readable either as merciful or as betrayal. It's one of the oldest of all stories, for ever since we began writing some 5,200 years back, we have etched our tablets, scrolls, and books with the same question: why evil? Why does the unimaginably traumatic happen?

The theological word for these stories is *theodicy*, which means a story about why God allows tragedy. Simplifying the way the question is typically framed, God is either (1) able to stop suffering but unwilling (and thus a monster) or (2) willing to stop suffering but unable (and thus not much of a God). The Bible's book of Job attempts to answer this dilemma, but there are many theodicies like it from ancient Mesopotamia. In the story, Job is a righteous man who in a single day, and for no fault of his own, loses his wealth and children to bandits and natural disasters. We are told it was because of a deal between a God and a satan. The Hebrew term *ha-satan* translates to "the adversary" or "the accuser," and it doesn't mean a devil (the devil isn't much of a figure in Jewish theology) so much as it means something like a prosecutor. The satan makes a bet with God, assuming Job would betray his God once happiness was gone. When disaster strikes Job's family, he isn't told about the bet; he simply must cope with the inexplicable. Like all too many sad times in our lives, Job has three friends who resolutely stay by his side only to suggest reasons he deserved his pain. Their three diverging explanations make the story so interesting even today.

Job is not the first theodicy. If several earlier Mesopotamian stories were crafted along similar story lines, what might the book of Job be saying that hadn't already been said? When asking why the big Other allows suf-fering, there is a big catch; asking why the gods (in the plural) allow horrors is different from asking why God (in the singular) does the same. When asked about the gods, destruction might happen because one god went to war with another, and the human being was caught in the crossfire as col-lateral damage. Perhaps the person who suffers worshiped the wrong gods or inadequately sacrificed to the right gods, and the gods are angry. The gods of polytheisms are always angry. We have a peculiar desire to see the universe as condemning us. But the question of theodicy in monotheism is more difficult, because all the responsibility comes down to a single actor.

Let's make this more difficult. Scholars typically think of the book of Job as combining two stories. It wasn't written by one person all at once, and it probably wasn't entirely finished in one century. There is a section of prose at the beginning and end of the book of Job, without which the poetic conversation between Job and his three friends (which makes up the bulk of the book) would not make sense. If we were to delete Job's arguments with his friends, we would still have a complete story of simple prose. We would simply go from Job's loss to Job's reward by God, but we wouldn't have the arguments with his friends that make the book so interesting for the question: why evil?

Our best guess is there was an original story modeled on earlier Mesopotamian theodicies, and then the bulk of the text was added during Judah's exile in Babylon in the sixth century BCE. In Babylon, the Jewish scribes were exposed to more stories and problems at the hands of Babylon and Persia, and they took foreign stories for their own. It was in the same period were the bulk of the Torah and Writings were being formed into a Bible. Another clue to the construction comes from the framing of the text. While the tribes named in the book's setting come from the days of Abraham, the use of the name YHWH for the God reveals the book was finalized much later. Whereas the narrator for the book of Job uses the later name YHWH for God, the characters in the story use more archaic names (Elohim, El Shaddai, etc.). It took quite some time for the two gods YHWH (in the south) and Elohim (in the north) to become a single God all re-maining Jews worshiped. It's also worth noting the ancient Israelites were henotheists, meaning they believed in many gods but only sacrificed to one God (either YHWH or Elohim, depending on if they lived in the south or north). It was not until the sacking of Jerusalem and the exile of Judah to Babylon that the ancient Hebrew religion became monotheistic. When they were exiled and no longer had access to their temple, the remaining Jews began to compile their scrolls into a single Bible, which would become the central focus point for organizing their faith. It was in this period of exile in Babylon, when the Hebrew Bible was being redacted and organized as a coherent collection of scrolls, that the book of Job was being further developed. A more sophisticated monotheism developed, but it had everything to do with the traumatic destruction of their temple. They adapted by becoming monotheists, and as we've said, monotheism is where the problem of evil becomes immeasurably more complicated.

Let us step into this strange amalgamation of stories. The satan approaches God in his court after scouring the earth. Without any prompting, God asks the satan if he has considered Job, a man whose devotion is unparalleled, and the satan takes up the challenge to make the poor servant Job reject his faith. Throughout the entire story, Job never finds out about this gamble between heavenly actors, which is the source of all his troubles.

In the first challenge, Job's wealth was destroyed and his children were all killed. When he did not revolt against God (who seems to feel more pride than pity), the satan returned to inflict sores upon Job's body. The only family Job had left was a wife who feels her husband is less a righteous man and more a fool for refusing to curse God and die. Foolish or not, Job turned inward and uttered the refrain now etched into our books as either (1) the epitome of grace and devotion or (2) the most troubling inability to see an abusive relationship for what it is: "The LORD gave and the LORD has taken away. Blessed be the name of the LORD."[3]

The big Other gives, the big Other takes. Blessed be the Name-of-the-Father. After Job loses his family and possessions, what follows is the poetic section added much later, a space where Job's three friends (and eventually a fourth) sit with him to make sense of why this has happened to him. Remember again how nowhere in the story does Job ever learn of the hellish gamble made in the skies above him. His friends are at first conciliatory and despondent, but with each turn of the conversation the argument becomes more and more one where Job *must* have deserved the trauma he suffers.

The explanations are as brutal as they are timeless. The friends accused Job in so many ways, but the accusations really came down to three groups: (1) suffering as punishment, (2) suffering as opportunity, and (3) denial of suffering.[4] These three explanations are still with us today, and

---

3. Job 1:21 (NASB).

4. I am indebted to James T. Butler's 2012 course at Fuller Theological Seminary for

they arise every time a friend desires to explain away our suffering. The explanations are meant to be helpful, but they rarely are.

First, Job is told to accept his fault, for he *must* have done something to offend God and deserve punishment. What, Job, have you done to deserve this? You had it coming, didn't you? Second, his friends suggest his suffering is actually a teaching moment, and Job is told to humble himself and embrace the opportunity to grow. Why aren't you thankful for the chance to spread your wings and rise above this? Why would you doubt God's plans for you? Third, Job's pain is dismissed as a self-centeredness. Don't others have it worse than you? What kind of narcissist draws such attention to himself?! His friends point to the poor and insist the starving orphan would desire nothing more than to trade places with him.

The three explanations show up in nearly every case of our suffering today, but are they not also the entire justification for our suffering under the system of neoliberal capitalism? The first explanation of suffering becomes "You are poor because you don't work hard enough." The second explanation becomes "You should be working to better yourself." And the third explanation becomes a dismissive, "You have it better than most! Why complain of being part of the downtrodden 99 percent when, compared with most of the world, you are the top 1 percent?!" Each of these explanations tries to mitigate suffering without changing anything, and curiously enough, we seem content with these explanations. Perhaps it really is because we are not creatures who desire to know but instead creatures who desire. We only desire knowledge inasmuch as it helps us get what we (think we) desire.

We saw a strange example of this contentment not to know with the Great Recession. We suffered, and we were told we should pull ourselves up by our bootstraps. We should suffer austerity and work harder. We Millennials were told we were clearly lazy, because we didn't make as much money as our parents and grandparents who spent decades eviscerating every mechanism keeping wages livable. We might guess most Americans would claim they have a decent grasp of why the economy crashed, but the answers are always nebulous—corruption, bad investments, evil men on Wall Street—rather than specific. Blaming the nebulous (yet visible) boogeyman allows the true causes to stay embedded in the system for which we voted. In short, if we don't know the precise meaning of the phrase "credit default

---

shaping the way I read Job, especially with regard to the separation of these three timeless explanations.

swaps on tranches of synthetic collateralized debt obligations," then we really don't yet understand the specifics of the crash. Those aren't words many of us know, and perhaps nobody truly understands them (including the bankers who cashed in on the scheme). The meaning of all those words, and the world economy they crashed, could be understood with only a few minutes of reading online, but we are content not to know.[5] In the same way, Job blessed the name of the Lord without ever desiring to know about the heavenly gamble that ruined his life.

Whether the gods are punishing us, teaching us, or perhaps if the gods have seen fit to harm others more—whatever the case, we're expected to humble ourselves and stay docile in moments of unrest and anguish. Our culture begs us to adopt a humble Stockholm Syndrome and thank it for the opportunity to suffer. Or at the very least we are expected not to draw attention to the meaninglessness of suffering. Over time, the arguments began to wear on Job, carving away his defenses until he started to agree that he perhaps deserved his trauma.

At this curious moment, rather than giving account, God entered the final scene out of a thunderstorm and said what had to be said: "Will the one who contends with the Almighty correct him? . . . Let him who accuses God answer him! Brace yourself like a man; I will question you, and you shall answer me."[6] The big Other had little intention for mercy. The speech of YHWH at the end of all arguments is nothing sort of a wandering, confused attack against the universe. It is what the theologian G. K. Chesterton called a moment where God himself seems to become an atheist, for rather than admitting to Job the secret gamble made with his life, God offers little more than rhetorical theatrics.[7] YHWH asks Job if he's considered the behemoth or whether Job was present when the foundations of the earth were laid. It is less an answer to the meaning of suffering and more a protest against even the possibility of meaning-making. Žižek renders God's speech as such: Look, Job, you think you have problems? Look at what I have to account for! It is a maddening speech, but after the diatribe Job fell to the ground and repented. It remains unclear of precisely what he even needed to repent.

---

5. For a very accessible introduction to the dynamics of the Great Recession, I recommend Lewis, *The Big Short*.

6. Job 40:2–7 (NIV).

7. The reference to Chesterton and much of my reading of the book of Job is indebted to Slavoj Žižek. See Žižek, "Dialectical Clarity Versus the Misty Conceit of Paradox."

In the end, the story ends happily in the same way the story of the prodigal son ends happily, that is to say, not as happy as it seems upon the first reading. Job's wealth is restored, and he has more children. Who would ever tell a parent who lost a child that all is now well simply because she had another child? On a closer reading, the final prose section at the very end of the book reads more like a thinly veiled threat. These too could be taken from Job. The righteous and the orthodox are forever in the service of the big Other, one who will never give account.

So there are multiple ways people read this story. Some find in Job the hope for the hopeless moment, a reason to remain faithful to a God who gives and takes away, though they always hope more giving will follow the taking. At the polar opposite extreme, the reading I find more helpful is one where suffering gets no serious explanation. There are questions for which every orthodoxy fails. If you ask, "Why did this unspeakable trauma happen to me?," I prefer a more problematic yet honest reading of Job saying nothing beyond: there is no good answer, and don't ever trust someone who tries to make coherent sense out of trauma. Perhaps the gods are punishing or teaching us, or perhaps others have it worse, but really all explanations will break down. If our theodicies and theologies make coherent sense out of suffering, then what we have is not God but an idol. The advantage of an idol is that it's always waiting in its expected place, holding our anxiety at bay.

Tiers of Trauma and the Rituals Covering Anxiety

Questions of whether our convictions are idolatrous leads right back to our confrontation with our own anxieties. In *The Courage to Be*, the theologian Paul Tillich said we have been writing the history of three types of anxiety: the ontic, the moral, and the spiritual.[8] First, we feel ontic anxiety over our questions of ontological being, or, in other words, we feel this type of anxiety at the realization we have a fate called death. We experience ontic anxiety because we are fragile creatures with blood that spills, bones that break, and hearts that give out. Second, we feel moral anxiety when we aren't sure how we measure up, whether we are good or bad, and whether we deserve the lives we have. Finally, we feel spiritual anxiety over questions of ultimate meaning and fears of meaninglessness. These anxieties are universal in each human being, but each of us negotiates them with the

8. See chapter 2 of Tillich, *The Courage to Be*.

full force of creativity, symbolism, and denial. It was out of anxiety that the gods awoke.

According to Tillich, each of these anxieties sits along a spectrum from relative to absolute. We feel ontic anxiety relatively when we consider our fate, but we shall experience it absolutely at death. We feel moral anxiety relatively when we feel guilty, and we feel it absolutely when we are condemned and cast out. We feel spiritual anxiety relatively when we ask whether our lives will have any real significance, and we feel its absolutely crushing force when we conclude our lives are truly meaningless. As a theologian, Tillich noticed human beings take these anxieties and organize them around rituals and symbols to blockade our fears.[9] So every ritual emerged from anxiety?

A symbol means different things in different circumstances. A painting of a crucifix means one thing for a group of scholars studying how Christians understood the death of Christ in some region at some point in the past. The same crucifix, Tillich rightly suggests, means something entirely different when gazed upon by the parent who just lost a child. The Eucharist means one thing when theologians debate transubstantiation; taking the bread and wine means another thing to the single parent who was just kicked out of her apartment. A symbol begins as one thing and mutates in each circumstance, but, if Tillich was right, we can be sure every symbol, ritual, and creed has at its base the primal impulse of anxiety. The symbol organizes anxiety and makes it useful.

We can think of symbolism as being made up of three levels: the Imaginary perception, the Symbolic underneath, and the Real behind it all.[10] When I use these terms, the Imaginary is the only one that is conscious; the other two are unconscious. The Symbolic is everything about our experiences shaping the way we deal with the Real, and by Real I don't just mean reality as such but, further, I'm referring to the traumatic experiences intruding upon us regardless of whether they are based in reality. Speaking as a psychoanalyst, Lacan used to say, "The gods are in the Real,"[11]

---

9. Excellent explanations of the differences between signs and symbols, as well as the argument that rituals organize anxiety, can be found in Tillich, "The Meaning and Justification of Religious Symbols," "The Religious Symbol / Symbol and Knowledge," and "Existential Analyses and Religious Symbols."

10. If you prefer a far more complex and sophisticated examination of the Imaginary, Symbolic, and Real, I use these terms in my previous book *God Is Unconscious*.

11. Quote modified from the original (the text does not capitalize real), Lacan, *The Four Fundamental Concepts of Psychoanalysis*, 45.

but, of course, he did not believe in many gods. Instead, the gods are representative figures intruding upon our worlds and filtered through the Symbolic (cultural expectations, cognition structured by language) to arrive at an Imaginary version (the gods as they are concretely described in scrolls and songs). The Imaginary is whatever we perceive, whether accurate or erroneous. Error is always in the conscious, for the unconscious never lies.

At the Imaginary level, we have a way we perceive the world to be, and our perceptions are always fleeting. In the earlier story of the girl who lost her parents, she was many things at the Imaginary level—a daughter, a team player, a driven personality, a good person—but, in a manner of speaking, she was only one of these things at a time. When she was participating in a sport, she thought of herself as a team player, and when she was at school she thought of herself as a good student. The relationship of the Imaginary to the Symbolic underneath is like a person standing beside an ocean. Suppose we were to kneel down to scoop up a fistful of water, sand, and sediment. We might arrogantly insist the handful is really all the ocean is, and then a moment later we cast the sediment back down and scoop up another. The second handful would have different pebbles or shells. Suppose we continued this process day after day, each time falsely thinking what we saw in our hands was what the ocean was really like. Our Imaginary identities and perceptions are just like this—they are one thing one moment and cast aside as we have a new thought. They have little to do with the depths of the ocean underneath.

With the example of the crucifix, we suggested it could serve one Imaginary purpose when studied for its theology, though the theologian will interpret the cross's meaning to be whatever she unconsciously expects it to mean. The same cross means something entirely different to the parent who has suffered the loss of a child, when the Real cuts through any Symbolic expectations she has and thereby produces a new meaning at the Imaginary level. If Tillich was right in claiming symbolism is always a response to traumatic anxiety, then perhaps we could be so humble as to abandon the misguided claim that theology (or any symbolically loaded construct) is ever merely rational. On the contrary, theology (if it actually has anything to contribute) is an Imaginary by-product of the brutal irruption of the Real into our mundane, unconscious expectations, and it should produce powerful ways for us to think about our anxiety. Theologies worth hearing are always infused with the traumatic, with the Real. They embrace their source in anxiety, because anxiety is the all-too-human condition. If theology stays safely within the expectations of orthodoxy, it has nothing important to say.

A friend of mine is a hospital chaplain. He sees the most brutal things that can happen to human bodies, and he counsels the families gathered at the emergency room. Only the trauma of the Real brings a family to an emergency room. He tells me an interesting thing happens when family gets hit by traumatic moments, namely, they repeat the same three explanations from the story of Job. They imagine they are being punished, or meant to learn something, or they think they don't deserve to complain. The families will tell him "Everything happens for a reason," but how, as a chaplain, does my friend respond?

For whatever brutal reason, our society tends to pressure a victim to rethink what happened. In the moment of anxious trauma (Real), we don't yet know how to process it at the Imaginary level. How we eventually process it will have a great deal to do with how we were raised, who our friends are, and what experiences we've had. If our Symbolic formation is supportive, we will arrive at a vastly different conclusion than we would if we feel we deserved pain. But our stories are fragile, and it is often sadly the case that long after we've come to peace with a painful event, someone pressures us to rethink how we might have been at fault. In other words, even if our Symbolic is supportive, a new voice might intrude and cause us to re-interpret the same event in a much worse way. We might heal and become unhealthy again, but it isn't because we didn't adequately deal with pain the first time. Instead, we often heal and suffer again because we allow in a voice that didn't deserve to speak.

We are forever on a precipice; we are one personal catastrophe away from reorganizing everything we believe. Only the worst of chaplains would decide to correct abstract theological interpretations while a family deals with pain. The only reason to correct would be if interpretation was causing immediate harm. Amidst trauma, we intuitively understand how the correct abstraction is insignificant. What matters is the successful organization of anxiety. We understand the most sophisticated philosophy has no power next to the simplest word ameliorating suffering. The Imaginary is supported by the Symbolic construction underneath, but the Imaginary is always one traumatic moment away from realigning altogether. A theology resisting change, a political posture prohibited from evolving, an academic discipline stunted in its growth, or a culture demanding a return to tradition—all these are like the bad parent who does not allow the child to mature along the path of the prodigal. It is like the idol mistaken for a God. It is the orthodoxy mistaken for righteousness. It is the false security mistaken for truth. We speak nonsense at full volume for years, and some are content to always speak nonsense at full volume for their whole lives.

From the Garden to the Prison

Nonsense is difficult to eradicate, because nonsense is all we've ever known. It's been said all theology begins as mysticism, so let us explore a Buddhist parable of how religion begins.[12] In this story, an elder teacher gathered his disciples every morning in the monastery's courtyard, and he poured his years of wisdom into his students day after day. The teacher carried on uninterrupted until the day a small cat wandered through the circle and distracted from the day's lesson. The lead student decided to tie the cat to a tree for the remainder of the lesson. When the cat returned the next day, they resolved to simply tie up the cat every day before the lesson and release it afterward.

After years of tying and releasing the cat during lessons, the elder passed away. The students continued to gather to reflect on his teaching, but they also continued as well to tie up the cat, which became as much a part of their ritual as their gathering for learning. The cat symbolized the elder in their minds, reminding the students of his slight irritation and their laughter together. Eventually the cat died as well, and the continuation of their ritual obviously required they purchase a new cat to tie to the tree each morning.

Generations of cats and generations of disciples came and went until, after hundreds of years of the daily ritual, the tree itself died and crashed to the ground. The monastery planted a new tree in the courtyard, and they continued to tie their new generations of feline friends. After a thousand years, the scholars began writing lengthy treatises on the theological significance of tying cats to trees. Councils were held to debate competing theories of why we should tie cats to trees, and disagreements caused the monastery split in turmoil.

This is how theology begins. Theology is the attempt to capture an intrusive object with precise words, but we haven't the slightest clue of

12. I must thank Peter Rollins for introducing me to this parable of the teacher and the cat. This Buddhist parable appears with many deviations of detail, and my retelling modifies the story further.

the object's depth (or our own). The object we symbolize and idealize is wrapped up in our trauma. The Real is filtered through Symbolic constructions, which then yield our Imaginary-level picture of how the universe works. The problem is that anxiety, truth, events, and the traumatic always contain more than what we can put into words. Our attempts to put words around the indescribable is always excessive and misdirected, and our theorizing leaves a misremembering that makes the original object seem like more than it really was. The third chapter of Genesis told us this much.

What better story examines the desire for a non-existent object than the fall of Adam and Eve? In this primordial myth, a bite of fruit symbolizes both (1) a real object (the fruit, nourishment) but also (2) the excess we try to capture (God's knowledge). The fruit had a power over the couple precisely because it was prohibited. The story is not simply about rebellion, sins, and taboos; it also shows the oldest storytellers already understood the human tendency to guard and misremember the taboo by creating new rules.

When the serpent spoke to Eve, it asked whether it is true they couldn't eat of a certain tree. What makes the story suggest something about how theologies gain traction (just as in the story of the elder and the cat) is that Eve does not understand the prohibition. Or more to the point, she, on her own volition, expanded the prohibition. We see the prohibition, we feel its anxiety, and we expand the prohibition to protect ourselves from crossing the line. Eve did not quite understand the prohibition, for God had only commanded the couple not to eat of the tree. Still, when the serpent asked its question, she added something else: "or even touch it."

The most effective prohibition would be the one that needn't be externally enforced. If we have a conscience keeping us from murdering, we won't need the homicide detective's investigation. If a mother teaches her child hitting his friend was wrong, he will begin to expand the prohibition against hitting to all people. If we are ticketed for speeding, we will regulate our speed even when no police are present. If our taxes might be audited, we might be less inclined to lie on our forms. The conscience is the imagined gaze of the big Other. But we also need outlets for our repression. If we are expected to obey our employers, we need a workers' lounge where we can complain just enough about the boss to let off our steam. If drivers shouldn't exceed ninety miles per hour on the highway, the authorities will set the speed limit at seventy-five and allow us to exceed it by a small margin. All of culture's rules depend on (1) our submission to prohibitions, which leads to (2a) expanding the prohibitions and/or (2b) breaking the prohibition in authorized ways.

The tree itself is interesting for its name, the Tree of the Knowledge of Good and Evil. The first prohibition in Genesis was not simply against sinning but, further, against knowing what would constitute sin in the first place. It's about the beginning of culture, for early in our prehistory there must have come a moment when our instinctual impulses for violence and self-preservation became tinged with something else. All of the sudden, an early *homo sapiens* swiped food from another, and the two locked eyes with something more than simple aggression; there was now a sense of moral indignation.

With this initial moral indignation came all the potential for culture. As Nietzsche suggested, the terminology *good* and *evil* entered the conversation, and we'd forever live in the aftermath. In a sense, it is when the Word became incarnated that things started going badly.[13] But what can we learn about the history of theologies (and their officially authorized orthodox versions) through this story of Adam and Eve?

Let us consider Genesis's story of Adam and Eve expanding prohibitions in comparison with the history of an interesting prison devised in the nineteenth century.[14] It was the brainchild of Jeremy Bentham, and his prison was designed in a circular fashion around a central guard tower. Each of the circular floors was stacked atop another. Each prison cell had one barred window facing out into the world and another facing inward toward the central guard tower. Each cell was fully illuminated with the day's light; anyone watching from the guard tower could see the entire cell, and the prisoner had nowhere to hide.

There was another catch. The guard tower in the center of the circular complex had windows with darkened glass or slats. The prisoner in each cell could never know if he was being watched at any given moment, but he was constantly aware he might possibly have eyes watching him.

---

13. This is a paraphrase of something Jacques Lacan once wrote, his point being that language and the expectations of culture turned us into something different than an animal. His more vulgar quote, which is both a reference to psychoanalysis and the incarnation of *logos* in the Gospel of John, reads as such: "It is when the Word is incarnated that things really start going badly. Man is no longer at all happy, he no longer resembles at all a little dog who wags his tail. . . . He no longer resembles anything. He is ravaged by the Word." Lacan, *Triumph of Religion*, 74.

14. Michel Foucault is responsible for these insights on the panopticon prison and the regulation of human behavior. See Foucault, *Discipline and Punish*.

Consider the difference between the old norm where police walked the streets and the more common practice today of police hiding behind some object in a vehicle shooting radar at the cars passing by. What is the difference between (1) knowing we are being watched and (2) knowing the possibility of being watched? When there is a prohibition, we do not simply avoid the prohibited activity. There's a distinct difference between knowing when we are or aren't being watched and, on the other hand, being unsure. We speed along in our vehicle every day and transgress the prohibited limit (by the slight yet expected amount of five or ten miles per hour), but we impose a limit on ourselves because there is always the anxious *possibility* we might be watched and caught.

In Bentham's circular prison, the prisoner might be watched every moment or ignored all day long, but the effect is the same. Escape becomes impossible, but beyond this, the interesting thing is rather how the prisoner no longer even attempts escape. The impossibility of a prisoner knowing if guards are watching makes his scheming irrelevant. In fact, we could even imagine a scenario in which there were no guards in the darkened tower at all. If the prisoner still consciously imagines he is being watched, he will unconsciously guard his own behavior.

This is the effect of anxiety, and this is the genesis of theology. The prisoner imagines an all-seeing gaze will catch his every attempt to transgress, so he polices his own boundaries by never attempting escape. In the same way, Adam and Eve were aware of a prohibition, and prohibition naturally raised the matter of self-limiting.

Given the prohibition against eating the fruit of the Tree of the Knowledge of Good and Evil, they could easily assume merely tasting the fruit was prohibited as well. So it's best not to even touch the fruit. What Eve said to the serpent about not being allowed to touch the forbidden fruit was not merely a mistake, for it was a natural self-policing or guarding act, which generates all our behavior. Guarding is the beginning of orthodoxy, generated from anxiety and the borders we dare not reconsider.

This chapter began with a story of a cynical evangelist called Marjoe who accidentally exposed the greatest fears of all the established theologians. The fear is that those who are paid to speak a certain selection of theological words just might do so, even if we don't find those orthodoxies believable. Those leaders who no longer believe—but are still commanded to sign statements of belief, use correct insider language, and behave a certain way—will do what they are paid to do. Or more directly, they will act out the role we pay them to play.

The orthodox guardians of Truth fear their game will be exposed as a ruse, nothing more than a treatise on the theological significance of tying cats to trees or useless explanations for why Job suffered. Orthodoxy fears it will be exposed as an empty series of prohibitions with no basis in reality. It fears it will be exposed as nothing more than a response to anxiety. Out of this fear, it restricts any radical thinking which might break open the barriers of enclosure. Orthodoxy encloses, domesticates, and commodifies everything in its reach into something feeling more safe.

Epistemic and theological safety is attractive, for illusions of safety stave off anxiety. Safety ensures us we needn't rethink our world, and it restricts suspicions concerning critical flaws. Again, in the same way the body desires homeostasis, the mind desires epistemic stasis, and we desire to change things just enough so things remain basically the same. We make minor adjustments to our theologies, politics, definitions, and habits, but the goal always seems to be the repetition of what is not working. It all ends up as the chimney sweeping of a staged theater.

When we speak with a friend who seems caught in a destructive life cycle even though she expresses every desire to break the pattern, we intuitively know the habits will continue because her habits provide her some obscene, covert pleasure. She may not acknowledge the unconscious pleasure, but we tend to understand people will continue to do what they have always done. We aren't surprised when people do something self-destructive, but rather the surprise is when people do something breaking with normal patterns. Even when we do not recognize it, we derive an obscene, covert pleasure from the repetition of what does not work. Once more, religion is all about pleasure.

Underneath all the rituals and formulas, there lies anxiety. The gatekeepers of every orthodoxy are the same. Today, theology doesn't work (at least not in its popular iterations). It is militant and patriarchal, sexist and violent, oppressive and coercive, but the gatekeepers tell us the problem is that we are not militant enough. They say we need more patriarchy, more capital, more conformity to social norms, and certainly less critical thinking. They are wrong, and they will soon take their rightful place as a laughable footnote to a better history. Radical thought counteracts orthodoxies of every kind with this message: those deeply held and well-concealed suspicions will not go away by doubling down on what doesn't work, for your anxieties about what doesn't work are right on the mark. We nevertheless repeat our broken habits, because we enjoy being ill.

The Dark Ages

A few hundred years from now, the exhaustion of the planet has led to the decay of society. Like the last Dark Ages, currency nearly goes out of circulation, the climate is chaotic, and governments lose the capacity to provide. Every person has their opinion of what should be done to regain some semblance of control, but the opinions are always free of content, reflection, or freeing potential. The universities disband, and the libraries shutter their doors.

The remaining teachers will gather together and decide so many years of exploration, discovery, and knowledge shouldn't be lost. However lost the human mind may be in the New Dark Age, they will determine our achievements merit preservation. The teachers will resolve to build an ivory tower and stow away safely with their books. They will raise new generations of teachers and make new discoveries until such a time when society reawakens and desires knowledge again.

They will gather together the mathematicians and the scientists, the scholars of literature and history. They will collect experts in every language and culture, compile a list of holy books and artifacts, gather technologies and technicians, and secure themselves in their tower. There will be no lock on the door, because it won't be necessary. Wanderers would be welcomed, but humanity won't have the appetite. The teachers will wait out the storm of destruction as long as need be in the hopes they might return to a world hungering for critical thought.

Theologians and philosophers will be there as well, but only of a certain variety. They will be those who do the bidding of the Master and not the Masses, and these thinkers will be cynics, ascetics, and orthodox. They will carry on their crafty debates for a thousand years without looking out the window.

One of them will be a monk who, after years of dedicated study, decides he should leave the tower and wander off into the world. His colleagues will caution him, "Our friend, you will be torn apart by the crowds, and your knowledge will be destroyed."

The monk will reply, "Perhaps, but while many of you know things that shall come back to life in the new epoch, I haven't anything stored in my mind that needs preservation."

"You cannot be serious," the others will counter. "Who else knows the Scriptures and the traditions? Without you we'll have no record of religion."

The monk shall sigh with the exasperation of one whose life has come to meaninglessness: "I hope you are right. What use is teaching without learning? You say I'll be torn apart and my knowledge destroyed?—it would be a small act of mercy."

9 What Our Four Names Betray

If this New Dark Age scenario came to pass, a great many disciplines would merit preservation for their own sake. Mathematics, sciences, literature, and even philosophy would deserve preservation, but I want to argue—specifically as a theologian and scholar of religion—that religion is not among them. Theology is usually better if sophisticated but irrelevant if incommunicable. In a previous book, I phrased the problem this way: "The university discourse isolates itself from common parlance, and in so doing . . . the human sciences outlive their usefulness by forging their servitude to the master's technocracy."[1] What a cumbersome way to say something I consider so dear! In many ways, this book is my effort to rectify my personal criticism of my own work. None of this matters much if it cannot translate to the masses who haven't the time to spend years on end studying theoretical niches. Sophistication, like simplicity, has its limits, and the ability of an idea to comfort us is no guarantee of the idea's truth.

Three Theologies: Vernacular, Academic, and Critical

After so many years of study, I still find it difficult to describe the actual aims and nature of the fields to which I've committed myself. They are abstract, and they speak indirectly, and to many this suggests they aren't necessary. Indeed, there are many forms of theology across religious traditions that we don't need at all, and I have very limited respect for theologies imagining they speak directly and philosophies claiming final answers. Ultimately,

1. DeLay, *God Is Unconscious*, 124–25.

136

philosophy and theology only helps the masses if they work to un-conceal. The idea isn't original to me. The philosopher Martin Heidegger said we should rethink the very notion of *alethia* ("truth") by returning to its Greek origins.[2] Rather than truth, a more accurate translation of *alethia* would be the term *un-concealing*. What would it mean to think of a philosophical theology as a type of un-concealing?

Heidegger used the example of Van Gogh's painting of a peasant's shoes.[3] It's remarkable such a gifted artist would paint such dull items over and over again. We wouldn't consider a painting art unless the it evoked something beyond the ordinary use value of shoes. What turns the mundane into art is the way a worn-out shoe suggests a hard life, few resources, and the awful conditions of poverty ironically portrayed upon a canvas that would sell for millions. It's never the items themselves but the reality beyond those items (realities specifically never pictured in the pieces themselves) making it art. Art designates the *beyond* of the image, and this is what it means to un-concealing. Likewise, Heidegger suggests we think of poetry as projective saying, for it creates alternatives out of the common. Then the task of critical thinking isn't to merely describe—let us leave to science and mathematics what can be described—but to un-conceal the realities behind, above, and inside what we see. A radicalized theology shouldn't concern itself with destroying heresies and misguided ideas; those ideas will kill themselves in due time. Instead, radical thought embraces the outsider's perspective and dedicates itself to un-concealing the insidious causes of whatever passes for popular ideology. In almost every case throughout history, the popular ideas are those foisted upon the masses by the masters who prefer their servants stay in the dark.

I am arguing there are three broad kinds of theology at work today. The Vernacular exists for the masses, the Academic for the scholars, and the Critical for both the masses and the scholars alike. The first is what we see all around us. It is in the churches, bookstores, and blogs, and it's both our security in a dire moment as well as fodder for pointless speculation among those who have too much time on their hands. This is the theology of the Vernacular, a word derived from the Latin word meaning domestic or slave (*verna*). It is the *language of the people,* and—if Marx was right—it is also their opium. The Vernacular can be revolutionary or regressive, but if the master allows it to exist, you can bet it is regressive. Put differently,

2. Heidegger, "On the Essence of Truth."
3. Heidegger, "The Origin of the Work of Art."

if economy works with a theology, or if a political party marries itself to a theology, or even if the dominant religious culture approves and feels no critique, it is the worst version of Vernacular theology. Of course, in Marx's day, opium was not an illicit drug but instead a medicinal pain reliever. It treated a symptom, never the cause.

There is also a realm of Academic theology taught in the academies and seminaries. It is sophisticated and complex, but it rarely reaches the shelves of the bookstore for mass consumption. Aside from the heaviest readers, most would only come into contact with Academic theology on the off chance their pastor worked it into a sermon. Though sophisticated, Academic theology is a recluse, and recluses rarely change societies. So in addition to the Vernacular theology of the masses and the Academic theology of the university and seminary, my question is whether there can be such a thing as a Critical theology opening up the boundaries of orthodoxies in a way that liberates the masses. It would speak with the rigor of the scholar while listening to the margins, but rather than communicating for scholars alone it would write itself accessibly for the benefit of the people. Can we hold sophisticated ideas that also aid our actually existing realities?

The task of un-concealing starts with this question: what isn't working well? The sister of this question is this: why are we anxious? Anxiety doesn't lie, and it tells us where we have a problem we'd likely prefer to ignore. When we identify an idea that simply doesn't work in the real world, it doesn't mean we necessarily know the correct answer. The correct answer is always evolving as we identify new ideas that don't work. We won't arrive at the finally correct conclusion, but it is enough to begin by locating problems. We should always be mid-thought, traversing unworkable fantasies.

As this book draws toward a conclusion, let's push further into the realm of mixed interests and concealed logics co-opting theology. We should develop one last schema to think about the individuals and the whole. We've explored schemas of simplicity to complexity along with cynicism and foolishness. We've explored how our own perspectives mix, match, and conflict with those who lead. So let us now go about thinking through a schema for how this process emerges. Let's suppose every idea fits within a certain message, a certain logic or ordering, and we shall explore the messages of (1) the Master, (2) the Masses, (3) the University, and (4) the Analyst.[4] Lest is should appear the University or Analyst is the

---

4. I am inspired here by Jacques Lacan's four discourses (University, Master, Hysteric, and Analyst), which I consider one of the most important and under-appreciated

protagonist of my schema, let us be clear: only the Masses ultimately matter. Only those who need liberation ever matter in any book worth reading.

Multiple Political Moralities

Before getting to this in terms of theology, let us step back into the different ways the same message gets itself heard in different ways. Psychologist Jonathan Haidt created a moral foundations theory of politics.[5] He describes a series of values and examines their different prioritization by liberals and conservatives. These values are:

1. Care/Harm: Others should be protected even when they cannot or will not protect themselves.

2. Fairness/Cheating: Rules should protect everyone equally and discourage unfair advantages.

3. Liberty/Oppression: Society should be organized to maximize freedom.

4. In-Group Loyalty/Betrayal: Fidelity to the tribe and its traditions should be maintained.

5. Authority/Subversion: Those in power over us are to be respected and obeyed.

6. Sanctity/Degradation: Certain objects or behaviors should be avoided.

Haidt likens these to taste receptors, and while liberals mainly taste the first three, conservatives have a broader palate including all six flavors. To be clear, he's interested in how certain groups see these as distinctly *moral* values, while other groups see them as (perhaps) ideal yet not moral. For example, all parents will prefer their child obey them. Certain parents will allow their child to disobey if the child is expressing herself or maturing. These parents might allow disobedience because they prioritize care (more than authority). However, the parent seeing obedience to authority as a moral value in itself will punish disobedience strictly.

---

contributions to political theory in the twentieth century. See Lacan, *The Other Side of Psychoanalysis.*

5. I am far too simply summarizing years of Haidt's research. I highly recommend Haidt, *The Righteous Mind.*

For another few examples, consider how when Edward Snowden revealed in 2013 that the United States government was collecting meta-data and email contents from all its citizens, the question in dispute became: is he a traitor or hero? Snowden felt citizens had the right to know their emails were being read, sexual photographs being viewed, and interactions being monitored, but not everyone agreed. Those who see in-group loyalty as a primary moral value might say yes, he is a traitor. Those who prioritize liberty over in-group loyalty would say no, he is not. Or consider how debates about gun laws exhibit arguments between liberty and care. If there is an irreducible conflict between the freedom to own guns and the inevitable violence done with weapons, how do we decide whose rights to prioritize? And finally, while we might think of *sanctity* as a conservative feature (namely, sexuality), is not the emphasis on ethical food an example of sanctity on the Left?

Even in cases wherein a whole group holds the same values, Haidt concluded we hold those values relatively rather than equally. You and I likely agree that equality is a virtue, but we might disagree on how far society should go to ensure equality. For example, someone who holds a high value on both fairness and sanctity might feel conflicted about marriage equality if they feel everyone should have the right to marry (valuing liberty and fairness), but marriage is defined by her faith (valuing sanctity and authority). How do we weigh our values and dish out judgements? Haidt's psychological experiments show liberals tend to prioritize the first three values (care, fairness, and liberty), while conservatives place a lower but more equally distributed value on all six. This is not to say a conservative is more moral (which is a matter for ethics), but instead we see how conservatives consider many problems to be moral whereas a liberal wouldn't consider the same scenario a moral problem. So a liberal will argue for equality (fairness) without realizing the argument doesn't settle the matter for a conservative, since, for the conservative, equality clashes with tradition (in-group loyalty, authority). A conservative argues for personal rights (liberty) as if it's enough to settle a question for a liberal who recognizes the harm (care) done by certain rights. In short, we end up talking past each other not simply because we hold different positions but because those positions are attached to quantitatively and qualitatively different values. I'm arguing theology has a number of different modes (messages, logics, modes of discourse), and we can analyze what a theology is doing by thinking through how it fits within a broader message.

There is no simple solution to this predicament of values, and we'll find no cure-all for deadlocked arguments. But neither is it helpful to cast aside our need for more honest conversation. We still have the option of framing those differences, thinking through schemas of what the different values are and what interests are served. Just as God asked the primordial couple who told them they had no clothes, we need to learn to ask: who told us to see the world this way, and why did they frame their demands in this way?

The philosopher G. W. F. Hegel wrote of the conflict between lords and their bondsmen as being a life-and-death struggle to acquire recognition.[6] The struggle is always lop-sided, for the bondsman has everything to gain in terms of freedom (even if risking his life), while the lord is only a master if he keeps his slaves. Until those who are oppressed feel they have nothing left to lose, the system maintains perpetual repetition. We have to have eyes to see before we can stop an oppression machine. It's at the precise moment when nothing is off the table that those in power must take matters seriously.

In many ways, what Hegel described is still our struggle today, for a great many things in the world need to change but never do. We lament conundrums of values and money, hopes and fears, terrorism and climate change, equalities and restrictions, and in the background of it all there is always a theology. Marx rightly observed that money and commodities contain a theologically fetishized dimension. We install trust in a piece of green paper or the pixilated number on a bank account screen, and we'd rather not think about the nature of this trust or why and how the system could implode altogether in a cataclysmic recession. Put differently, theology is about more than gods; it is about how we invest trust. The way we defend the unquestionability of debt repayment is not so different than how we defend our orthodox theologies. Everything is tinged with theological dimensions. Every claim is a deceptive fetish. Every belief calls itself the Truth.

But as Marx also correctly observed, the criticism of religion is the beginning of all criticism. He said the criticism of heaven should transform into a criticism of the earth, the criticism of religion into criticism of law, and the criticism of theology into the criticism of politics. It's not enough to keep a critique in its place; we should always be expanding our questions

6. The dialectic of lord and bondsman can be found in Hegel, *Phenomenology of Spirit*.

outward. It's not that we should criticize theology into the ground—a futile effort if there ever was one. Instead, a question in one space should lead to questions in other spaces. I suspect everyone reading a book like this already knows how questioning religion ends in questioning everything else. We said it in the first chapter: we might think we are only asking about the creation myths of Genesis, but in short order we are asking about the minimum wage. In short, questioning the Master Signifier begins the deconstruction of everything following from that Master Signifier.

We ready to confront my final schema of logics, or identity-generating discourses: the *Master*, the *Masses*, the *University*, and the *Analyst*.[7] To overlap these four logics with the three theologies I introduced earlier, recall the Vernacular theology for the Masses, an Academic theology for the University scholars, and perhaps a radically Critical theology hoping to aid both the Masses and the University. A Critical theology should work from the discourse of the Analyst, which aims not to instruct the Masses (which is what the University discourse does) so much as it aims to listen to and liberate the desire of the Masses. I only consider a theology to truly matter if it helps to liberate the Masses and un-conceal the enslavement posed by the Master. So a Critical theology (which is usually rife with academic jargon) must ultimately speak in the Vernacular—the language of the people—if it has anything to contribute. The logics of the Master, Masses, University, and Analyst are all thrown into a world that is ordered to serve the Master. Whether we think of the Master as the economy in general or capitalism in particular, if we instead think of the Master as the president or CEO, or if the Master is whoever is in control (perhaps the white Evangelical), everything in the real world is tailored for the service of the Master.[8] No Master wants his oppressed creatures to think for themselves, and we likely all feel the pressure today *against* critical thought. Where there is money and power, there is a Master. If theology has anything left to say, it must notice there's a Master begging it to sit quietly, to think the right things, to vote the right ways, to purchase the right products, and ultimately to

---

7. While the separation of theologies into three groups (Vernacular, Academic, and Critical) is my idea, the rest is indebted to Jacques Lacan. I am modeling my three theologies, respectively, on Lacan's discourses of the Hysteric/Masses, University, and Analyst. I changed the word Hysteric to Masses, and I will explain this change in the section on the Masses.

8. For a truly fascinating theory of resonance between the master of Wall Street and the subservience of American Evangelicalism, see Connolly, *Capitalism and Christianity, American Style*.

foolishly trust the correct cynics. The Master prefers we remain fools. Let us burn down those demands.

The Master Speaking the Language of Power

The advantage of putting full faith in a God is that (no matter how unsure or unhappy we are) we assume there is a big Other out there doing the knowing and enjoying for us. We imagine if we can simply align our desires with the ultimate desirer, then our desires will be good enough because they are God's own desires. But when God is no longer Master, who took the place? Who are our gods today, and what do they want? Indeed, we might imagine the answer to this question would tell us what we should want, but it would really only tell us what someone else wants us to want.

The Master acts as the Master Signifier for everyone else. If I am called American, then my book is an American book. If I live under neoliberal capitalism, all my choices are already capitalist by the force of circumstance, however much I'd like to imagine otherwise. If I am called Christian, then my thinking is presumably Christian thought. The Master Signifier is the light by which we see all else, that which shades our Imaginary picture with its deceptive hues and which clouds our judgement. The Master today is wealthy and powerful, the one we seek to emulate as the pinnacle of achievement. He is on our advertisements and covered in our journalism. He creates jobs for the rest of us, and he tells us who should lead. His threats are backed up by the funding he threatens to withdraw, and his money is the reason we go to work. The Master is not a singular *he*, but instead the Master is anyone who occupies this position of power. The Master infects everyone—occasionally the Master is a person, but the logic of the Master always fills our hearts as the goal we desire to become. Our concept of a Master, by its very definition, is a way of thinking about who wins, who we emulate, and to whom we submit.

For an example from feudal Europe, the lord was the Master of the peasant Masses. The lord would divide up his land and allot portions of land to a peasant family for farming. The lord would tell the peasants they should work the land five days per week for themselves, one day per week for the lord, and then they should rest on the Sabbath. In this arrangement called feudalism, the peasants accepted they'd work one day per week for the lord, because the lord was gracious and merciful to give his land away. If the peasant were to suspiciously fall ill on the day he was supposed to work for the lord, there would be hell to pay. Thusly so, the lord could arrange shifts of labor so, every single day, a group of peasants worked his land and produced his crops. The point is that the peasant must work for the lord, and the peasant sees this as justice. Marx observed that feudalism is not so different than capitalism today, for today we contract our labor and see it as normal. I am admittedly oversimplifying his crucial insight, but he called this reallocation of created value (from the laborer to the owner) *surplus exploitation*. An economy is only capitalist if it's mostly organized around a mode of production wherein surplus is exploited and relocated. We thank employers for the opportunity they provide as so-called job creators. When we tell our employers we'll work for X hours per day for Y dollars, we know the employer will only hire us if we are producing more value than what he pays. If the employer pays us for all the value of our work, then he makes no profit and has no incentive to hire us. After all, he isn't a job creator out of the goodness of his own heart.

We don't think of what we produce at our jobs as our own property. Just as the peasant gave some of her labor to her lord, we give the excess of our work to the Master. He takes our work and turns a profit. The Master calls the shots and determines society. We desire to emulate him because of our faith that he is good (or at least effective, productive, and perhaps intelligent). Just as nobody in the feudal world was lord unless he reigned over a horde of peasants, the Master today is only a master because of our faith and desire. Faith in the Master is a theology of its own. Without trust, he—like the money he commands—is nothing.

The Master relates to the rest of us as subjects, as laborers, as followers, and as tools. We are the means of production, the source of income, and the machine for his power. The Master is no fool, for he knows his position is precarious at best; he must keep the corporate machine working (and working in his favor). The Master does not care how a machine works anymore than a factory owner cares how the assembly line produces its vehicles. The Master does not care *how* things work, only that they *do* work. If it turns out badly with harsh lives for the Masses, why should the Master care?

The Masses sacrifice, and the Master reaps the reward. Out of every product we create and he sells for a little more than it took to make, he scalps a bit of money and calls it profit. Perhaps it's no sin in the short term, but over time the Master becomes larger and larger. His profits, companies, campaigns, and powers grow, and it all comes from the slight excess he gathers into an aggregate multitude. We would rebel if we realized this, so the Master did something brilliant and reframed his machinations as a moral imperative to obey.

In the Middle Ages and up until the Reformation in the sixteenth century, scholars and kings argued for something we'd find abhorrent today. They called it the "divine right of kings," a fanciful way of claiming God himself gave kings their authority. If God gave us the king, who are we to question God by rejecting the king's authority? I'd argue that the divine right of kings didn't really go away; it just went underground. The political theorist Carl Schmitt even said, "All significant concepts of the modern theory of the state are secularized theological concepts."[9] We don't usually say God gave a president or employer his authority, but we readily accept a moral responsibility to do the Master's bidding.

Plato once challenged the definition of "the good" as telling the truth and paying our debts, because our ethical actions can be used by another for evil. Perhaps the Master's most powerful move was getting us to think of debt as an internalized responsibility each of us owes to the Master. We are told to respect our authorities, for to show too little respect means there is something deficient and rebellious in us. We submit, because we are convinced submission is our moral responsibility. Is it even considered particularly odd when a poor mother would choose to pay her utility bills before feeding her children? Even worse, the Master purchased the support of the churches by telling us God himself established this moral/economic arrangement, as if God was concerned with the authority of the factory manager or the politician.

But what does the Master seek? What does he want, and can it be satisfied? Well, in addition to the clear lines of power, money, privilege, and social order, the Master cannot say precisely to what ends he desires. The wealthy still go to therapy, because the endless pursuit of pleasure acquisition reveals how every pleasure gives less than it promises. The Master goes to the psychotherapist for the same reason the child, by Christmas afternoon, no longer cares about the toys she has wanted for months. Water quenches thirst temporarily, but we become thirsty again.

Recall the story of Diogenes where he told Alexander the Great their only difference was that, while both ultimately wanted to relax, Diogenes would simply prefer to skip conquest and relax today. Diogenes did not adopt the logic of the Master. If Alexander heard the message rightly, he'd have realized the homeless madman was living out the ultimate dream of

---

9. Schmitt, *Political Theology*, 36.

the emperor. There's an excess to every drive that cannot be satiated or satisfied by the acquisition of what we think we desire. The Master's production works in the short term, but it does not resolve the gap between the object (wealth, power, fame) he seeks and the sense of fulfillment the object promises (but always fails to provide).

Psychologists have noticed how when people win lotteries, the very wealth they believe will solve their problems turns out to create an explosion of new problems. Friendships fray, divorce papers are served, and bankruptcy is often the final result. The elevation to Master—even of a new Master who swears they will be a different kind of Master—does not resolve the problem of the supposed-missing-object. The supposed-missing-object (fulfillment, satisfaction, no more need) is the remainder that cannot be satisfied by acquisition of power. But rare is the person who sees through this charade and rejects the logic of the Master altogether.

The result of this Master's logic is that people are churned up, used, abused, dispossessed, disenfranchised, impoverished, and even then they still end up desiring to become a Master. Occasionally one of us does indeed become the wealthy Master, which condemns us to become part of the same unending machine. We will be sitting in the psychoanalyst's clinic in no time, because we will become thirsty again. But most of the time, the worker remains poor and falsely believes the Master has access to a kind of wisdom, know-how, or satisfaction we do not have.

If too few see through the deceptive logic of the Master, the effect is that the Masses keep voting, praying, and cheering in the Master's favor. And again, the Master is not concerned with how things work, only that they do work. No matter what means the Master must deploy to co-opt the interests of the Masses—whether co-opting their religion, ethics, education, or family values—the Master must keep us cheering for him to win.

The Masses Protesting or Submitting to Power

How could theology ever counter such deception? The Master's power depends on a theological trust, so how do the rest of us respond? There are really only two ways to respond, namely, submission and revolt. I am deviating from Lacan and my previous work, where what I am about to describe was what psychoanalysis called the Hysteric's discourse. I alter the term to Masses for a number of reasons, not least of which is the potentially misogynistic implications of the word hysteria. In psychoanalytic theory, the hysteric is the defiant agency holding all the real knowledge, and thus he or she is most suited to throw off the conditions demanding submission. Like the earlier example of the left-wing fool, the hysteric provokes and makes demands, even if those demands can't be fulfilled, because the hysteric knows things could go better. This is the positive version of hysteria, or what I'm calling the logic of the Masses. But there is a negative form as well, which submits to the Master and imagines the repetition of what doesn't work (in relationships, economies, and religion) will eventually work out. It won't. In the negative, submissive form, the Masses become populists. Populism is often nothing but purely regressive ideology, empty rhetoric, and directionless movement. It doesn't matter whether the cause energizing the base is the support for xenophobia and white supremacy, the so-called traditional family values of the Religious Right, or whatever else—the Master prefers the Masses be populist, because populists unwittingly support the Master's profit margins.

According to the political theorist Ernesto Laclau, populism depends on *empty signifiers* which can then deploy *floating signifiers* as needed.[10] The empty signifier is a type of Master Signifier which is only given meaning by the populist group supporting it. Traditionally, "the people" was the key empty signifier of populism, and the leader (or demagogue) would rally the crowds and convince them they (and they alone) were the ones who should hold control. In America today, the classic term "the people" has been almost entirely eclipsed by "real Americans," a term claiming a type of collective authority even though it tends only to designate those who are white, Protestant, and patriotic. After the populist group organizes under an empty signifier, the leaders can deploy floating signifiers (pro-business, anti-corruption), which are more specific and yet somehow always vague. One can win elections by making a key issue out of something that's never really defined. The floating signifier must always revolve around the empty signifier like a moon in the gravitational field of a planet. The populist party must balance between a logic of difference (the specific interests and demands of those within the populist coalition) and a logic of equivalence (emphasis on what each special interest has in common), for to emphasize either difference or equivalence will collapse the populist's momentum and turn it into simple authoritarianism or democracy. In America today, the Masters have nearly completed their co-opting of religious populism, and

10. To read further on these ideas, I highly recommend Laclau, *On Populist Reason.*

thus there isn't anyone in America left unscathed by the theological trust the populist Masses instill in the Master.

If there are both regressive, populist versions of the Masses and revolting, liberating versions of the Masses as well, how would a theology look when it supports revolt? How could the language of the Vernacular be deployed to counter the false gods of the Master? Let's take an example from history. When Martin Luther launched the Reformation by nailing the Nintey-five Theses against indulgences to the Wittenberg castle door on October 31, 1517, he still believed a simple debate about theology was the deepest issue. We like to think a debate is simply about ideas, but in reality ideas can't transfer without the technologies delivering them. In 500 CE, a mere 12,000 books were created each century in Europe. By 1800 CE, the number would balloon to more than a million. Books are nothing without literacy. When Luther was writing in the sixteenth century, only one in four city dwellers (and one in twenty rural folk) could read in their own native language.[11] It was a time when theology, like any academic discipline, was carried out purely in Latin. It was a language nobody but the scholar spoke or read. One way to think of Luther's success is a transition from an academic Academic theology to a Vernacular theology for the Masses, the Vernacular being what desires to incite real change rather than theological speculation.

Luther developed relationships with a whole network of publishers sympathetic to his cause. When Johanne Gutenberg introduced Europe to the printing press in the 1440s, it revolutionized the production of books and pamphlets. Instead of hiring an expensive scribe to copy a book by hand (which meant books were only for the educated and ultra-wealthy), Gutenberg's press allowed a single book to be copied hundreds of times in a month. The invention spread across Europe in a sporadic pattern. Only the largest cities tended to have a printing press by the time of the Reformation, but Luther's home country of Germany was different from the rest of Europe. For whatever reason, Germany had printing presses operating in nearly every city, even in smaller towns.

A large reason that Luther succeeded was language and printing. While the Catholic scholars tended to debate in Latin, Luther would write his argument out for them in Latin, immediately translate it into German, and then have his affiliate publishers spread his message across the countryside

11. To read further on the rise in printing books, see Buringh and Van Zanden, "Charting the 'Rise of the West.'"

for the commoners to read. Luther could preach in Wittenberg and then, within a week, have the sermon printed in the influential city of Augsburg. His message was being preached across Germany almost simultaneously in cities to which he'd never traveled. For those who couldn't read, he produced wood cuts and images to communicate his attacks without words. For those who would gather at taverns and read aloud to their comrades, Luther wrote with sharp wit and hyperbolic style that would have had the rowdy crowds cheering at his latest threat against Pope Leo X. While Luther was as angry, well-educated, and vituperative as anyone they'd ever seen, he was writing his pamphlets and translating his New Testament in the common language. It wasn't just his writing in German; it was his vernacular style. He wanted to be read by the Masses.

If the Master desires to control the Masses, the best thing he can do is outlaw critical thought. In George Orwell's famous book *1984*, the government creates Newspeak to control the language's capacity to think non-sanctioned thoughts. If the government found a word to be subversive, it would simply rewrite the word so it communicated less. Similarly in the 1930s, the populist Nazi propaganda intentionally kept itself simple so as not to trigger intellectual awakening. In America today, the defunding of literature and humanities departments in universities has a similar motive (if unintentional). There isn't much funding for philosophy, but there is a never-ending flow of cash for science, technology, engineering, and mathematics. The focus on the technical and the lack of interest in the philosophical leads to humanity as machine rather than humanity as human. If the Masses need awakening, we must learn to speak in the Vernacular.

The Masses are left in a precarious quandary. They are caught between the interests of the Master and their own desire for liberation and control over their lives. Increasingly today, our choice is between making money and doing good, but is it much of a choice when the game is rigged?

An interesting figure arises to promise the Masses their freedom, and we explored this figure earlier with the story of the journalist confronting the cynical candidate who didn't honestly believe much. Populism is the name political scientists give for a type of awakening of the Masses, but populism is usually regressive and devoid of anything but rage. Knowledge has no place among those who desire to regress, and they will mock your critical thinking accordingly. However, if populism can take a liberating form (and I think it can), it will arm itself with information and desire for revolt. Political populism rewards the loudest and crudest leader, who always speaks in the common tongue, but there's no guarantee of whether the populist leader seeks good or ill. When he desires ill, the populist leader is merely serving the concealed interests of the Master. The populist leader uses nationalist, racist, or religiously bigoted language, and in this way he uses the Vernacular against the Masses—who nevertheless think him their savior. The preachers who support the cynical populist leader are also guilty of using the Vernacular against the Masses, and all of this serves the Master well enough.

In an earlier chapter, we discussed the Christian fundamentalist movement of the earlier twentieth century, and we saw it was largely funded by wealthy businessman with profits from the oil industry. No doubt many of the businessmen were sincere in their belief, but in retrospect we see their money and belief created a devastating movement. It gave rise to an apocalyptically cultish theology in the early twentieth century, which in the twenty-first century justifies the rampant abuse of the environment, support for endless war, and the harm of the poor and middle classes. In a very serious sense, oil money converted into fundamentalist theology, which in turn supported the careless use of more oil and the violence it demands.

Fundamentalism is the religious form of populism par excellence. Fundamentalism is pure ideology—the drive of belief once all reasonable excuses for belief are gone. It is pure desire without knowledge. Fundamentalism is a populism seeking to enjoy, and we are creatures that find enjoyment in self-harm. For example, when the West gazed upon the horror of 9/11, the media focused on a questionable belief not found in the Qur'an or any significant Muslim text, namely, the belief that seventy-two virgins awaited the suicide bombers in paradise. American media needed to believe this was the motivating factor, because American Christians cannot think in non-hypocritical terms. We believe an act supposedly serving a God must have ulterior motives; we do not like to think someone could directly believe so much in their faith that suicide is a form of enjoyment. Both Islamic and Christian fundamentalists are obsessed with enjoyment, though neither would admit it. The Islamic fundamentalist abhors the decadence of the West and desires women to cover themselves, for he desires to lust in secret (just as the Christian fundamentalist desires) rather than celebrate sexuality in the open media.[12] Evangelical purity culture does the same. American Christians are quick to locate religion as the source of violence

12. The examples of terrorism and the different relationships with enjoyment in Islam and Christianity come from McGowan, *Enjoying What We Don't Have*.

in another culture, but we haven't the eyes to see the religious motivations for our own foreign policy. We say steadfast support for Israel is just good policy, and the Middle East should always be invaded to protect persecuted Christians, but many still imagine it hasn't anything to do with blind faith.

I once watched a video of a ministry operating in United States military in which soldiers sang lyrics dripping with violence, and I pictured the horror so many Americans would feel if the location and religion were different. Fundamentalisms are all the same, but wherever a fundamentalism is in power, its adherents don't have to believe directly. They can believe with hypocrisy and feign horror at the extremists of other faiths who believe so deeply they sacrifice their lives. Empowered fundamentalism never considers how a minority fundamentalism mirrors its own desires. The American fundamentalist, who has all the real power in society, wants to keep his Christianity secluded to Sunday so he can live as if their is no God on the other six days. He desires to suppress sexuality for others, because he is frustrated himself. Other-hatred is so very often nothing but an externalized self-hatred. Though lust and power are the furthest things from the fundamentalist's lips, fundamentalism is all about concealed desires.

The danger of populism is the downside of writing in the Vernacular. The Vernacular can be misunderstood, devoid of reality, or taken to unexpected conclusions. When Luther proclaimed the "priesthood of all believers," he didn't expect the peasants to take him so seriously as to revolt against their feudal lords in the Peasants' Revolt (which is why Luther ultimately supported the violent suppression of the peasants). But populism and fundamentalism, like any symptom, tell us the Masses have a flaw. Populism is not a coherent, correct answer to a problem, but it does tell us a problem is there.

In the realm of politics and religion alike, populism refers to ideology, a form without substance, a pure drive to serve at the support the Masters we imagine will support our values. We seldom consider how the Master behaves once in power. And so we support the anti-war candidate because we are anti-war, and we vote for him again even though he launched a new war. Or we support the anti-abortion candidate if we are pro-life, even though his policies do nothing to address the economic and social conditions creating abortion. Or we support so-called commonsense fixes to economic policy, even though the fix leads to more debt and lower wages. Or we support so-called biblical values, because we know the world is changing and we'd rather not think about why. If ideology is form without substance, ideologues are those who can't be convinced their way of seeing the world has a critical flaw.

On the other hand, the Masses have all the real power. The Masses can call foul on theologies that don't work and cast out those who betray us. We have access to every bit of information ever gathered with only a moment's search on a smartphone, but the Masses can't do anything with information until they desire something beyond the desires of the Master.

Think of the predicament of teaching today under these conditions where, as we just said, all information is available online. Where teaching was once needed to transmit information from the one with knowledge to the one without knowledge, we today exist in a climate where the student sits with a laptop while the professor lectures. It is now the student who has access in the moment to information the professor does not have, but only an anti-intellectual person would say we will suddenly self-educate to such a degree that teachers are no longer necessary. The role of teaching today is not merely the transmission of fact but the construction of knowledge, for we need people who can organize information in new ways, trigger insights, and show people that what they need to know is what they largely already suspect (but don't know they know). Let's push further into this world of populism to think about how the Masses embrace their revolutionary potential.

Even before being a person, the Master is an idea to emulate. The Masses submit to the ideological game in hopes of acceptance into the fold. The Masses say the right things, believe the correct beliefs, self-identify the right way, and work the long hours. The Masses submit in every way demanded, and they do so in order to become the Master (an aim which will always be thwarted). We are nostalgic for pasts that never existed and paranoid of enemies that don't threaten us, and we are always begging for a populist to redirect our rightful rage against the wrong enemies. As Malcolm X famously put it, "If you aren't careful, the newspapers will have you hating the people being oppressed and loving the people who are doing the oppressing."[13]

The Masses sit in pews on a Sunday morning to praise a God who has supposedly ordained their harsh life, and they hear a sermon of how more even more submission is needed. Occasionally a sermon speaks the truth, and here is how we know a sermon speaks truth: the self-professed

13. Malcolm X, *Malcolm X Speaks*, 93.

guardians of Truth will reject the message, labeling the content as seditious and its speaker as immoral.

The Masses may become docile and submissive populists or revolting revolutionaries. The former wants to conserve the existing order (or go backwards), while the latter says our best days are still ahead (if only we might have ears to hear those who suffer). The truth is that the Masses are kept motivated by the very same excessive emptiness the Master buries deep in his soul. In the same way we always desire the supposed missing object, which itself never satisfies but only starts up the process of desire again, the ultimate truth for the Masses is that she has desires with both *submissive* and *revolutionary* potential. There is a world of difference between regression and liberation. Those who want to think differently—who sees the vanity and endless striving of the populist fundamentalism and Master it serves—might go to the University with the hope that freedom is within grasp.

The University Serving Power

Early on, I confessed coming from the part of America where people dare not think. It sounds dismissive to say, and yet when I visit home it is not unusual for me encounter an odd accusation: "You are learning too much for your own good." I'm continually amazed this gets said without a trace of irony, as if facts or critical thinking were a menace to society. But on the other hand, I understand this world as my home. I understand the disdain for being talked down to, the anxieties enmeshed in change, the fear we might discover our faith is farce, and—most of all—I understand the distaste for academic language so seemingly detached from reality. I'm no enemy of education, which is why I've invested years into degrees and niche scholarship. I'm also convinced nothing I study matters if it doesn't aid the broader public.

I suggested Martin Luther's Reformation might be thought of as a war of transition from Academic theology to a Vernacular theology for the Masses. We can easily imagine the peasant's distaste for the educated elite and their Latin works, but the educated elite still held a lofty position in the towns from which they hailed. Debates would rage throughout a far-off university in academic jargon, and then those ideas would spread when the student visited home. Once more, ideas only transfer to the people if they're put into the people's Vernacular.

We all know the University and its students who seek to rise above populism with insights based in years of learning. Learning is one of the most sublime desires, and we shouldn't ever denigrate it. The Master would love it if we dismissed education as unnecessary. Sure enough, the academics are my own tribe now. What I hope to argue is that there is a type of University thinker who isn't quite yet an Analyst, and it's a type of University thought that abandons its responsibility to the Masses and ultimately submits to the Master as well. This University thinker becomes trapped inside its own language until motion ceases. The University thinker might have earned her right to be an expert, but for every academic there is also a populist eager to preach his dangerously content-free clamoring to the Masses. In short, what we're calling the University thinker cannot communicate to the Masses and leaves an ideas vacuum the populist charlatan will exploit.

We also know people who style themselves as thinkers when, in fact, they have nothing to say. In such an age where we have nearly infinite opportunities to pour our ideas into the worlds of social media, there is no shortage of people who have convinced themselves they should speak simply because they can speak. I recently saw an article by a self-described theologian (who seems to have little training or reflective capacity) tell his readers the rise of ISIS was a sign of the end times. He further claimed Christians were the only thing stopping the world from descending into immorality, and he speculated that the anti-Christ would be gay. He previously said Obama might be the anti-Christ, but I suppose time ran out. When I read this kind of abysmally content-free opinion, I marvel at the level of paranoia and learning resistance that could make this self-styled expert seem attractive to readers. I marvel in the same way when I read those who dismiss the Black Lives Matter movement or the plight of Palestinians, because it shows that we think we get to have an opinion on someone else's pain. The clinical term for this is *narcissism*. Narcissism prefers the University never speak in the Vernacular.

There is a joke among philosophers: if you ever reach such an abstract argument that you decide you are not sitting in the room you are sitting in, then it's a good rule of thumb to assume you took a wrong turn in your logic. The same holds for theology: if your argument leads to a conflict with a field studying the phenomenon you are deciding, or if your thought is exactly what the Master prefers, it's a good rule of thumb to assume your theology has taken a wrong turn and overstepped its boundaries.

A culture of narcissism isn't the University's fault, but it played a part in the problem when it stopped speaking in the Vernacular. The University became obsessed with respectability and endowed chairs, with cutting costs and building campuses, with paying for sport while defunding the humanities. There are any number of examples, but they all boil down to this: the University started serving the Master. When the Master said it needed skills X, Y, and Z, the University looked across the campus and cut down the departments that didn't match. It boosted the dean's and coaches' salary while it cut the professor's tenure, and today three-fourths of professors are adjuncts contracted per semester for a salary that doesn't even reach the poverty line. At the same time, parents and students continue to pay skyrocketing costs without realizing their professors might be on food stamps. Under those conditions, did we expect the level of critical thinking to remain unharmed?

The University begins by advertising itself to the Masses as the place to come for knowledge acquisition. The University deploys its models, theorems, histories, philosophies, theologies, physics, and mathematics. After a few years, the University has churned out a newly enhanced worker. None of this is bad at all, and in fact this process of slow and productive learning is the way our society matures. The problem comes if the University has *only* produced a newly licensed job-filler for the use of the job creator. This too is necessary, but at some point we have to ask whether the University is *only* keeping the economic machine alive rather than unleashing human potential. Likewise, at some point we must ask: is the seminary producing a thoughtful priest or merely a deep-in-debt worker to carry out religious tasks? An Academic theology is suited to tasks, but a Critical theology revolts. Is learning becoming commodified such that learning only ultimately serves the Master?

Socrates said the unexamined life isn't worth living. I should be clear that I consider philosophy and theology (at least the type I'm describing) to be what everyone is interested in, whether they realize it or not. But there's a popular saying among Christian fundamentalists that captures the populist's perceived right to opinion without learning. The saying goes, "everyone should be a theologian," which has a certain truth while betraying the implementation of the truth. It is true everyone in a society ruled by Christian hegemony has a vested interest in learning theology. We also have a vested interest in learning about health, but nobody ever says "everyone should be a doctor." What the difference between "everyone should be a theologian" and "everyone should be a doctor" betrays is that the believer, quite without realizing it, thinks there is no real substance to study in one of them. Every religious person gets to be their own favorite theologian or philosopher, because we unconsciously assume the questions aren't serious at all. And why dedicate any serious time or attention to something so irrelevant as empty, opinionated speculation? We descend into a careless relativism where all opinions are equal, and this is most frequently seen in those who think themselves anti-relativists.

This relativist reduction is common when the theology of the Masses is actually serving the Master. It's toxic not only because it is a practice of hegemony—where those with privilege and power can unconsciously domineer the oppressed—but also because it exposes itself as a farce. The charlatan is a cynic who desires to take advantage of the fool, and the fool desires the lies of the charlatan.

We have a long tradition of theological learning in seminaries and universities, in monasteries high in the mountains and in practice on the developing country's streets. The tradition spans from the women mystics of the medieval era to the Latin American and black liberation theologies of today. There are whole traditions upsetting the boundaries of hegemony, the boundaries that always lie. It turns out there is indeed a depth to theology and philosophy opening up a space for us critical reflection. We should learn these traditions so as not to make the same mistakes our forbearers made.

What would it look like to think of schools, universities, books, community collectives, etc., that go *beyond* the reproduction of the Master's Signifier? What does it look like to adopt a theology that doesn't sit well with the Master's machine? We can be sure what it wouldn't look like: something that is accepted by the *status quo*. Cornel West provides an example of a path forward from the University toward the Analyst, or from the Academic to the Critical. West is a highly credentialed scholar who has taught at Princeton University and Union Seminary, and the breadth of his scholarly publications would fill up several pages. However, when speaking publicly he uses a prophetic style of language, which is just as accessible as that of his fundamentalist counterparts. He is a scholar also speaks the language of the Masses. It's a style of both learning and action, equally academic and prophetic. The powerful do not appreciate a figure such as West, because nothing he teaches will aid them in keeping the Masses docile. The prophetic voice never keeps anything docile. In short, he preaches from the lonely position of the Analyst.

The Analyst Desiring Liberation

The choice set before those who desire knowledge (which is unfortunately not so many of us) is between the bureaucracy of the University and the perceptive analysis of the Analyst. There is not a third option for those with eyes to see and ears to hear; there is only bureaucracy and analysis.

A Critical theology is a radical theology. One of my favorite philosophers of religion likes to say "God does not exist; God *insists*."[14] Another who was a psychoanalyst said, "In the end, only theologians can be truly atheistic, namely, those who speak of God."[15] Another who was a mystic asked what it mattered if a virgin gave birth to a God if we do not give birth to God today. Another who is a theologian says, if God is always on the side of the oppressed, "God is black."[16] At each and every turn, the Analyst incites the Masses's desire to think further. The Analyst is a radical critic—not one providing answers but instead seeing what doesn't work and putting dysfunction to use. It will be an aggressively Critical theology, because the Masses are being aggressively harmed.

Through these pages, we've repeatedly walked through the pivotal question: which is the symptom, and which is the cause? We instinctively understand some diseases can be treated for their symptoms only (such as the common cold), while for others the treatment of the symptom alone would prove fatal (such as a cancer). For whatever reason, we cast this knowledge out the window when it comes to addressing the most pressing social issues. We think it perfectly appropriate to ask the male about patriarchy, the Caucasian about the African American experience, the straight person about queer identity, the upper class about the problems plaguing the poor. The Analyst is the one who rejects this misguided dismissal of lived experiences and sees the symptom as evidence of a concealed cause. The Analyst listens to those on the underside of every hegemony. Only those who are oppressed truly understand the nature of oppression.

14. Read everything ever written by John D. Caputo. Start with Caputo, *The Insistence of God.*

15. Lacan, *Encore*, 45.

16. Read everything ever written by James Cone. Start with Cone, *God of the Oppressed.*

Just as the University brandishes knowledge accumulation as its insignia, the Analyst takes up the position of desire for liberation itself. Consider the case of someone going to analysis for the first time, who feels she needs some kind of help but is not yet convinced the analyst has the key to liberate her desires. The patient begins the clinical sessions by awkwardly testing and probing, asking what she is supposed to do or how free association is supposed to work. The psychoanalyst simply instructs the patient to say whatever comes to mind and begin talking—the conscious Imaginary does not quite know why life is not working out so well, but the same patient's unconscious Symbolic network knows everything there is to know. The Symbolic begins to speak out, first in dreams, slips of the tongue, and mistakes, which lead the patient to exclaim, "I didn't mean what I just said!" When we don't want to confront the truth, we guard and lie to ourselves.

When we lie to a friend when asked a difficult question, we feel the anxiety of hoping our friend doesn't detect the lie. But in a sense, what truly matters is not whether or not the friend detects the lie but instead whether we detect what have hidden from ourselves. The friend merely serves as a blank screen upon which we project a part of ourselves. We can then see our lies in the third person and see what we couldn't before see. The anxiety felt when we realize we are lying is a symptom, and if we seek to rectify the cause, we will listen to the symptom. It's the same with any oppression we'd rather not recognize.

The first step for those with privilege must be our learning how to listen to others without it. Nothing productive happens in psychotherapy until the patient becomes convinced the analyst is a subject-supposed-to-know with access to something she wants. The Analyst must represent this desire for liberation. Though the populist Masses are often happy to remain submissive, the desire for liberation lies dormant and awaiting within us all. We remain submissive because we don't know how to identify symptoms and causes, and we don't know how to identify these because we didn't learn to listen. The Analyst must learn a great deal, but she must also learn to speak in the Vernacular about the symptoms and causes plaguing us. If the Analyst can learn to speak in the Vernacular, a Critical theology emerges in revolt against the demand to submit.

A good psychoanalyst gives the patient a new Master Signifier, a new way to think about their overwhelming guilt. The good teacher says just enough to incite the student's desire to go home and learn more on her own. The good preacher stirs the heart with the recognition that no current order is the final, best order. Just as no law is the finally perfect Law, no current order is a kingdom of God. Just as no philosophy is the final, perfect logic, every question should lead to a new question. If a new Master Signifier is given to the people, new ways of thinking about the world might begin to unfold.

What does it mean to think of theology as for the Masses? I'm saying we have only the options of (1) reproducing what the Master desires or, instead, (2) producing something the Master does not want the people to know. Since Christianity hasn't learned much since the day of Christ, we can tell the difference between these two options by asking whether the self-professed guardians of Truth approve or disapprove. The guardians of Truth are charlatans and cynics, and they cling to their orthodoxy because they haven't anything valuable to say. Many among the University and the Masses promise knowledge, but they know fully well the anxiety they are hiding. The Analyst is the one for which no question is off limits, the one who begins by listening to the disenfranchised outsider, and the one who helps the Masses rethink the Master's command to see the world in such-and-such a way. Any theology with something to say will conflict with the power structures from which it emerges. It will conflict with its established theologians. It will conflict with its seminaries. It will conflict with its political parties. It will conflict with its economic arrangements. It will conflict with traditions of every kind. It will not sit well with orthodoxies.

Unfortunately, the outlook for theology is grim. Since religion is an inherently conservative way of thinking, it's not at all clear theology can survive without bowing to the power of tradition, force, and pleasure-seeking. Radicalization fills the streets with a South American liberation theology, the European universities with a critique of power, the Global South with a protest against capitalism, or North America with the death of God. Whenever there is radicalization, we will see a correspondingly intense institutional pushback.

I've had the pleasure of meeting a great number of thinkers who have shaped me, and one thing standing out to me with every meeting is that none of us possess any certainty we are on the correct path of thought. The Master is certain he is correct in all he does and speaks, but the University and the Analyst are always thinking in progress. And just as the difference between the University and Analyst can only be judged afterward by whether they actually help, our work of can only be judged in the long term.

Do not trust those who beg you not to think. Do not trust those who look down on your youth or your desire to learn. Do not assume that both sides always have a point, because it is not uncommon for one side to desire destruction. Do not trust those who lord their self-righteous piety or privilege over you. Do not fall into the trap of thinking the niceness of a person excuses the indefensibly awful views to which they demand you adhere. Do not listen to those who feel nostalgia for whitewashed, imaginary pasts. Do not trust those whose ideal world would visit immense harm upon the powerless. Do not trust the justification of "it's just the way things are" any more than you trust "the way things have always been." Do not trust those who feel their faith vindicated when they see the world getting worse. Do not trust someone who imagines they understand all their motives fully; we are such immensely clever beings who always hide our motives, even from ourselves. As the prophets have always said, a great many of us never acquired eyes to see or ears to hear. When you look upon the horizon and sense the flood of questions, do not hear those who'd prefer the rains never fall and the dam never breach. Whoever fears critical thinking has nothing to contribute, and we need not pretend otherwise.

What I'm firmly convinced of is that the Master is a cynic who desires to keep the fool in the dark. The nihilist Master does not care whether you become a populist or a student, a financier or a scholar, an entrepreneur or a worker, a religiously affiliated or a none-of-the-above, a conservative or liberal—he only desires to keep you a fool. The Master desires you to remain orthodox in view, paranoid in outlook, and nostalgic for a perfect society which never existed. Have nothing to do with it.

Epilogue

I found myself at a conference, the same mentioned in Kester Brewin's foreword, listening to a discussion tracing the rise of the national sovereignty during the Reformation to the climate's collapse under the weight of carbon. The global situation is, of course, quite dire among those who've read the future. I never learned her name, but one person stood to suggest something about hope and inevitability: "We are already saved, we are already dead, we are already someone else's fossil fuel."

It's really too simple to write a books about cynics and fools. Whether we think of the difference as a simple binary or sophisticated spectrum, the truth is we each contain our foolish beliefs and cynical deceptions. We like to imagine we are good, and we deplore the idea we are machines that eat and breathe and heat. We like to imagine our religions are lofty and sublime rather than a haphazard, mammalian adaptation to keep us alive. The natural question is whether any of it is true. A teacher once said this about it: "That [Christianity] is the true religion, as it claims, is not an excessive claim . . . when the true is examined closely, it's the worst that can be said about it. Once one enters into the register of the true, one can no longer exit it."[1]

I like this idea, because if I were to tell you exactly what I think—and to be sure, I've bared only a fraction of my honesty—it's only a matter of time before I'm proved a fool. Perhaps there is such a thing as genuine sacrifice and faith, an authenticity which isn't simply a vulgar, mammalian adaptation. If there were, I'm confident of this: this type of creativity would be part and parcel of our most destructive drives. We are only creative because we are also destructive. Our desire for the righteous orthodoxy, perfect relationship, or all-knowing leader is buried in our desire to repeat what never works. Perhaps we have a calling, and perhaps we'll let it rot. At any rate, if it serves the Master rather than the Masses, it should be left to perish.

1. Lacan, *Encore*, 107–8.

Acknowledgments

A book is a store of the author's experiences and the thoughts of oth-ers. I accumulated influences throughout my studies, and there are a great many names to which I'm indebted. Some of those names are listed in the text, and others hide in the background. The names lying prominently in the open are Jacques Lacan, Michel Foucault, Slavoj Žižek, Friedrich Nietzsche, Sigmund Freud, Karl Marx, and Paul Tillich. The names in the background are Judith Butler, Clayton Crockett, Todd McGowan, Ernesto Laclau, Louis Althusser, and Ingolf Dalferth. There are perhaps a hundred others. Though I have strived to keep jargon and names to a minimum in the interest of accessibility, please understand this book is an accumulation of the greater minds who have influenced me.

There are also those who have influenced me who I am honored to call friends. To Pete, for the comments on my manuscripts, for the endless conversations, and for everything that goes with being a co-laborer in a theoretical niche, I am ever grateful. To Clayton, a leading figure in psy-choanalysis and theology, thank you for encouraging me ever since I was a novice academic. It has made all the difference. To Kester, a man with no tolerance for bullshit and a deep desire to write the truth, what could I really say? You read both of my manuscripts before anyone else saw them, and your careful advice has made my work so much better. To Lauren, you suggested revisions as a trained psychologist, and you're also one of the best human beings I've had the pleasure of getting to know in the last couple of years. Thanks to Jesse once again for the beautiful cover art, and thanks to the terrific team at Cascade, who made the final production of this book effortless. My work is indebted to all of them, and the errors that remain in the text are mine alone.

The person behind all of this is Deven. A book is a work of love, so to speak. You are the editor, supporter, fixer, and tireless reworker of

everything I create. You laugh with me when I think I've been clear with examples that only make my jargon more opaque, and you've spent so many
hours with me in our favorite coffeehouses and bars as we rush to beat
deadlines. You see value in my work when I don't, and you encourage me to
keep going when I'd rather quit. You are my best friend.

Bibliography

Berinsky, Adam. "The Birthers Aren't Going Anywhere (An Update)." YouGov. Accessed June 18, 2016. https://today.yougov.com/news/2012/10/01/birthers-arent-going-anywhere-update/.

Berrigan, Daniel. *A Book of Parables*. New York: Seabury, 1977.

Breuer, Josef. "Anna O." In *The Freud Reader*, edited by Peter Gay, 60–78. New York: Norton, 1989.

Brewin, Kester. *Mutiny! Why We Love Pirates, and How They Can Save Us*. London: Vaux, 2012.

Buringh, Eltjo, and Jan Luiten Van Zanden. "Charting the 'Rise of the West': Manuscripts and Printed Books in Europe, a Long-Term Perspective from the Sixth through Eighteenth Centuries." *The Journal of Economic History* 69.2 (2009) 409–455. Accessed June 20, 2016. http://www.jstor.org/stable/40263962.

Caputo, John D. *The Insistence of God: A Theology of Perhaps*. Bloomington, IN: Indiana University Press, 2013.

———. "Proclaiming the Year of Jubilee: Thoughts on a Spectral Life." In *It Spooks: Living in Response to an Unheard Call*, edited by Erin Nichole Schendzielos, 12–47. Rapid City, SD: Shelter50, 2015.

Cone, James H. *God of the Oppressed*. Maryknoll, NY: Orbis, 2015.

Connolly, William E. *Capitalism and Christianity, American Style*. Durham, NC: Duke University Press, 2008.

Dawson, William James. "The Evangelism of Jesus." *Brooklyn Daily Eagle*, February 6, 1905. Accessed June 21, 2016. http://bklyn.newspapers.com/image/53931470/.

DeLay, Tad. *God Is Unconscious: Psychoanalysis and Theology*. Eugene, OR: Wipf and Stock, 2015.

Deleuze, Gilles, and Félix Guattari. *Anti-Oedipus: Capitalism and Schizophrenia*. Translated by Robert Hurley. New York: Penguin, 2009.

Derrida, Jacques. "Force of Law." In *Acts of Religion*, edited by Gil Anidjar, 228–98. New York: Routledge, 2010.

Dobbin, Robert, ed. *The Cynic Philosophers from Diogenes to Julian*. New York: Penguin Classics, 2012.

Erikson, Erik. H. *Young Man Luther: A Study in Psychoanalysis and History*. New York: Norton, 1993.

Freud, Sigmund. "Beyond the Pleasure Principle." In *The Freud Reader*, edited by Peter Gay, 594–626. New York: Norton, 1989.

———. "The Ego and the Id." In *The Freud Reader*, edited by Peter Gay, 631–58. New York: Norton, 1989.

———. *The Future of an Illusion*. Translated by W. D. Robson-Scott. Mansfield Centre, ON: Martino, 2011.

———. *Group Psychology and the Analysis of the Ego*. Translated by James Strachey. New York: Norton, 1959.

———. "Instincts and Their Vicissitudes." In *The Freud Reader*, edited by Peter Gay, 562–68. New York: Norton, 1989.

———. *Jokes and Their Relation to the Unconscious*. Translated by James Strachey. New York: Norton, 1960.

———. "Obsessive Actions and Religious Practices." In *The Freud Reader*, edited by Peter Gay, 429–36. New York: Norton, 1989.

———. "Repression." In *The Freud Reader*, edited by Peter Gay, 568–72. New York: Norton, 1989.

Foucault, Michel. *Discipline and Punish: The Birth of the Prison*. Translated by Alan Sheridan. New York: Vintage, 1995.

Foucault, Michel. *Power/Knowledge: Selected Interviews and Other Writings, 1972–1977*. Edited by Colin Gordon and translated by Colin Gordon, Leo Marshall, John Mepham, and Kate Soper. New York: Pantheon, 1980.

Graeber, David. *Debt: The First 5,000 Years*. New York: Melville House, 2011.

Haidt, Jonathan. *The Righteous Mind: Why Good People Are Divided by Politics and Religion*. New York: Vintage, 2013.

Hegel, G. W. F. *Phenomenology of Spirit*. Translated by A. A. Miller. New York: Oxford University Press, 1977.

Heidegger, Martin. "On the Essence of Truth." In *Basic Writings*, edited by David Ferrell Krell, 111–38. New York: Harper Perennial, 2008.

———. "The Origin of the Work of Art." In *Basic Writings*, edited by David Ferrell Krell, 139–212. New York: Harper Perennial, 2008.

Heschel, Abraham Joshua. *God In Search of Man: A Philosophy of Judaism*. New York: Farrar, Straus and Giroux, 1955.

Keeley, Brian L. "Of Conspiracy Theories." *The Journal of Philosophy* 96.3 (1999) 109–26. Accessed June 20, 2016. http://www.jstor.org/stable/2564659.

King, Martin Luther, Jr. "Letter from Birmingham Jail." Accessed June 21, 2016. http://kingencyclopedia.stanford.edu/kingweb/popular_requests/frequentdocs/birmingham.pdf.

Klinman-Silver, Cloe, et al. "Location, Location, Location: The Impact of Geolocation on Web Search Personalization." Northeastern University. Accessed July 24, 2016. http://www.ccs.neu.edu/home/amislove/publications/Geolocation-IMC.pdf.

Kuhn, Thomas S. *The Structure of Scientific Revolutions*. Chicago: University of Chicago Press, 1996.

Lacan, Jacques. *Anxiety: The Seminar of Jacques Lacan, Book X*. Edited by Jacques-Alain Miller and translated by A. R. Price. Malden, MA: Polity, 2014.

———. *Écrits: The First Complete Edition in English*. Translated by Bruce Fink. New York: Norton, 1996.

———. *The Ego in Freud's Theory and in the Technique of Psychoanalysis, 1954–1955: The Seminar of Jacques Lacan, Book II*. Edited by Jacques-Alain Miller and translated by Sylvana Tomaselli. New York: Norton, 1991.

————. *Encore, 1972–1973, On Feminine Sexuality, the Limits of Love and Knowledge: The Seminar of Jacques Lacan, Book XX*. Edited by Jacques-Alain Miller and translated by Bruce Fink. New York: Norton, 1998.

———— *The Ethics of Psychoanalysis, 1959–1960: The Seminar of Jacques Lacan, Book VII*. Edited by Jacques-Alain Miller and translated by Dennis Porter. New York: Norton, 1997.

————. *On the Names-of-the-Father*. Translated by Bruce Fink. Malden, MA: Polity, 2013.

————. *The Other Side of Psychoanalysis: The Seminar of Jacques Lacan, Book XVII*. Edited by Jacques-Alain Miller and translated by Russell Grigg. New York: Norton, 2007.

————. *The Triumph of Religion*. Translated by Bruce Fink. Malden, MA: Polity, 2013.

Laclau, Ernesto. *On Populist Reason*. New York: Verso, 2005.

Laertius, Diogenes. *Lives of the Philosophers*. Edited by A. Robert Caponigri. Chicago: Regnery, 1969.

Lewis, Michael. *The Big Short: Inside the Doomsday Machine*. New York: Norton, 2011.

Luther, Martin. "The Freedom of a Christian." In *Career of the Reformer: I*, edited by Harold J. Grimm and translated by A. W. Lambert, 327–77. Philadelphia: Fortress, 1957.

Malcolm X. *Malcolm X Speaks: Selected Speeches and Statements*. Edited by George Breitman. New York: Grove, 1990.

Marx, Karl. "A Contribution to the Critique of Hegel's Philosophy of Right: Introduction." Edited by Joseph O'Malley. Marxists Internet Archive. Accessed June 16, 2016. https://www.marxists.org/archive/marx/works/1843/critique-hpr/intro.htm.

————. "Theses on Feuerbach." In *The German Ideology*. Amherst: Prometheus, 1998.

McGowan, Todd. *Enjoying What We Don't Have: The Political Project of Psychoanalysis*. Lincoln, NE: University of Nebraska Press, 2013.

Nietzsche, Friedrich. *On the Genealogy of Morals | Ecce Homo*. Translated by Walter Kaufmann and R. J. Hollingdale. New York: Vintage, 1989.

Peretti, Jonah. "Capitalism and Schizophrenia: Contemporary Visual Culture and the Acceleration of Identity Formation/Dissolution." *Negations* 1 (1996). Accessed July 15, 2016. http://www.datawranglers.com/negations/issues/96w/96w_peretti.html.

Pew Research Center. "Public Sees a Future Full of Promise and Peril." Accessed June 17, 2016. http://www.people-press.org/2010/06/22/section-3-war-terrorism-and-global-trends/.

————. "U.S. Christians' Views on the Return of Christ." Accessed June 17, 2016. http://www.pewforum.org/2013/03/26/us-christians-views-on-the-return-of-christ/.

Plato. *The Republic*. Translated by Desmond Lee. New York: Penguin, 2003.

Rollins, Peter. *The Divine Magician: The Disappearance of Religion and the Discovery of Faith*. New York: Howard, 2015.

Schmitt, Carl. *Political Theology: Four Chapters on the Concept of Sovereignty*. Translated by George Schwab. Chicago: University of Chicago Press, 1985.

Scribner, R. W. "Incombustible Luther: The Image of the Reformer in Early Modern Germany." *Past & Present* 110 (1986) 38–68. Accessed June 30, 2016. http://www.jstor.org.ccl.idm.oclc.org/stable/650648.

Thornwell, James Henley. "The Rights and Duties of Masters." In *A Documentary History of Religion in America to 1877*, edited by Edwin S. Gaustad and Mark A. Noll, 538–41. Grand Rapids: Eerdmans, 2003.

Tillich, Paul. *The Courage to Be*. New Haven, CT: Yale University Press, 1952.

————. "Existential Analyses and Religious Symbols." In *Theological Writings*, edited by Gert Hummel. Vol. 6 of *Main Works*, edited by Carl Heinz Ratschow, 385–99. New York: De Gruyter, 1992.

————. "The Meaning and Justification of Religious Symbols." In *Writings in the Philosophy of Religion*, edited by John Clayton. Vol. 4 of *Main Works*, edited by Carl Heinz Ratschow, 415–20. New York: De Gruyter, 1987.

————. "The Religious Symbol / Symbol and Knowledge." In *Writings in the Philosophy of Religion*, edited by John Clayton. Vol. 4 of *Main Works*, edited by Carl Heinz Ratschow, 253–76. New York: De Gruyter, 1987.

Whitford, David M. "The Papal Antichrist: Martin Luther and the Underappreciated Influence of Lorenzo Valla." *Renaissance Quarterly* 61.1 (2008) 26–52. Accessed June 17, 2016. http://www.jstor.org/stable/10.1353/ren.2008.0027.

Žižek, Slavoj. *Did Somebody Say Totalitarianism? Five Interventions in the (Mis)use of a Notion*. New York: Verso, 2001.

————. "Dialectical Clarity Versus the Misty Conceit of Paradox." In *The Monstrosity of Christ: Paradox or Dialectic?*, edited by Creston Davis, 234–306. Cambridge, MA: MIT Press, 2009.

————. *How to Read Lacan*. New York: Norton, 2006.

————. "Paul and the Truth Event." In *Paul's New Moment: Continental Philosophy and the Future of Christian Theology*, edited by Creston Davis, 74–99. Grand Rapids: Brazos, 2010.

————. *The Puppet and the Dwarf: The Perverse Core of Christianity*. Cambridge: MIT Press, 2003.

————. "We Are Not Dreamers, We Are the Awakening From a Dream Which Is Turning Into a Nightmare." Verso. Accessed June 18, 2016. http://www.versobooks.com/blogs/736-slavoj-zizek-at-occupy-wall-street-we-are-not-dreamers-we-are-the-awakening-from-a-dream-which-is-turning-into-a-nightmare.

Made in the USA
Coppell, TX
22 December 2019

13669447R10106